Transport economics

Colin G. Bamford
University of Huddersfield

Second Edition

Series Editor
Bryan Hurl
Harrow School

Helen Buck
UGCJM.

Heinemann Educational Publishers
Halley Court, Jordan Hill, Oxford OX2 8EJ
a division of Reed Educational & Professional Publishing Ltd

OXFORD FLORENCE PRAGUE MADRID ATHENS
MELBOURNE AUCKLAND KUALA LUMPUR SINGAPORE
TOKYO IBADAN NAIROBI KAMPALA JOHANNESBURG
GABORONE PORTSMOUTH NH (US) CHICAGO MEXICO
CITY SAO PAULO

Heinemann is a registered trademark of Reed Educational &
Professional Publishing Ltd

First published in 1995
This edition published in 1998

02 01 00 99 98
10 9 8 7 6 5 4 3 2 1

British Library Cataloguing in Publication Data

ISBN 0 435 33042 X

Typeset and illustrated by Techtype Ltd
Printed and bound in Great Britain by Biddles Ltd, Guildford

Acknowledgements

I would like to thank Bryan Hurl for his comments on the first edition of the book and for his subsequent editing of this second edition. Thanks also to my colleague, Dr Tony Whiteing, for his contribution to the text of Chapter 3. My grateful thanks are also due to past and present students in the Department of Transport and Logistics at the University of Huddersfield who have given me the opportunity to teach them some of the topics in the book. Suzanne Scott deserves thanks for word-processing my revisions to the original manuscript, which she also produced for me. Finally, and not least, I should like to thank my wife Elisabeth and daughters, Emily and Alice, for allowing me the time to write. I hope I have not neglected them in the process.

The publishers would like to thank the following for permission to reproduce copyright material.

The Department of Transport, Environment and the Regions for the data on pp. 6, 7, 9, 10, 12, 15, 27; Eco-Logica Ltd. for the extract on p. 75; *The Economist* for the extracts on pp. 71, 74, © *The Economist*, London (6/12/97); EMAP Apex Publications Ltd. for the diagram on p. 62; Freight Transport Association for the data and extract on pp. 21, 27; Lord Hanson for the extract on p. 24; HMSO for the data on pp. 38, 46, 64–6, Crown copyright is reproduced with the permission of the Controller of Her Majesty's Stationery Office; *Huddersfield Daily Examiner* for the extract on p. 88; *The Independent* for the graphs on p. 17; London Examinations, A division of Edexcel Foundation, for the questions on pp. 18, 77; *Motor Transport* for the material on pp. 34, 84; Northern Examinations and Assessment Board for the questions on p. 33; The Office for National Statistics for the data on pp. 13, 14, 18; *Punch* for the cartoon on p. 23; © The Telegraph plc, London, 1997, for the map and extract on pp. 44, 78; The University of Cambridge Local Examinations Syndicate for the questions on pp. 9–10, 33–5, 47–8, 64–6, 77–8.

The publishers have made every effort to contact copyright holders. However, if any material has been incorrectly acknowledged, the publishers would be pleased to correct this at the earliest opportunity.

Contents

Preface

The new Labour government has already announced its intentions for transport: a positive, integrated transport policy which will grapple with Britain's universal, economic problem – of demand for roads outstripping supply. All the issues of road pricing, cost–benefit analysis and the outcome of the transport privatizations are covered here. In addition, the opportunity has been taken, in this new edition, to add a chapter on sustainable transport.

This volume is written by the Chief Examiner for the UCLES Modular Examination at A level, specifically for Module 4388 for which he is responsible.

Bryan Hurl
Series Editor

Introduction

We live in a world of change. Change is all around us and impacts heavily upon our daily lives. More specifically, since 1995 when the first edition of this book was published, there has been a very clear re-orientation of thinking towards the transport sector, not only by economists but by politicians of all the main parties in the UK. It is now generally recognized that a sea change in direction of national transport policy is inevitable. The transport crisis which we face cannot persist much longer.

It is clear from the forecasts of future transport demand, particularly for roads, that this demand will continue to outstrip supply at an ever-increasing rate. Given the many conflicting needs being placed upon public expenditure, the only way in which the problem can be addressed is through the acceptance and application of new approaches to transport policy, with a clear focus on 'sustainability'. These issues are discussed in a new final chapter on 'Transport for a sustainable future'.

Elsewhere, the remaining chapters have been

- modified to include the most up-to-date statistics available
- updated to take into account other aspects of transport change since 1995 – this particularly applies to Chapter 5 which now contains a fuller account of rail privatization and the impact of bus service deregulation.

This second edition contains five new data response questions and many additional new essay questions, all of which have been set since 1995 by the A level examination boards.

The emphasis of this book in all chapters is to apply the main principles of economic analysis to current transport problems and issues. Some basic knowledge of the theory of market economics and market failures is required in order to fully understand the specific transport application. To keep up to date, students are strongly encouraged to read a good newspaper, as the policy context is ever-changing; there is also an increasing range of material available on the Internet – the Department of the Environment, Transport and the Regions, for example, now has a comprehensive Web site. Educationally, the nature of the subject matter very much lends itself to a student-centred approach. Stimulus material is provided in the text in the form of boxed items – students could be encouraged to build up a similar collection of items for use in the classroom.

This book is intended for use by A level Economics students alongside a standard textbook. Like all books in the *Studies in the UK Economy* series, it is designed to provide a particular up-to-date perspective on an aspect of economic policy. It complements others in the series, particularly the latest editions of *Privatization and the Public Sector* and, to a lesser extent, *Green Economics* and *Equity, Efficiency and Market Failure*.

The book will be of particular relevance to students taking module 4388, Transport Economics, of the UCLES/CMAL A level Economics syllabus. Over the least two years I have been encouraged by the feedback I have received from teachers of this syllabus and have tried to take their comments into account where possible in this new edition.

Increasingly, though, transport topics are being examined in the linear and modular A level Economics syllabuses of all of the main examination boards, which is indicative of the accessible and topical nature of the subject matter. Such students will find Chapters 3, 5, 6 and 7 of particular relevance to their studies.

The book is also of relevance to those taking the professional examinations of the Chartered Institute of Transport and to undergraduate students studying transport economics for the first time. It has been produced to be entirely consistent with OCR's new A2.6 syllabus in Transport Economics.

Chapter One

The nature of transport economics

'Transport is civilisation.' Rudyard Kipling

═══

What is transport?

Transport is concerned with the movement of people and goods for a variety of personal and business purposes.

In studying transport movements, it is necessary to recognize two important but clearly interrelated elements, namely:

- the **infrastructure** – i.e. roads, railtrack, airspace and associated terminal facilities such as distribution centres, railway stations, ferry terminals and so on, on which movement takes place ór on which transport needs are met;
- the operation of transport vehicles – i.e. cars, lorries, trains, aircraft and vessels.

Making this distinction from the outset is important for the following reasons:

- Decisions on infrastructure are usually taken by the government (as is the case for roads), by the government indirectly (as was the case for railtrack and airports until recently), or by privately owned transport businesses (e.g. distribution centres).
- Decisions on transport operations are in the main taken by private businesses, with little or no government involvement apart from there being an overall regulatory framework within which such operations can take place.

Consequently, there is a complex situation within transport. This can cause particular problems when students look at transport statistics and information.

Returning to the basic definition above, we can make the following observations:

- *Transport demand takes place over space and time.* All journeys are made over a particular distance, between start and end points, and take a particular amount of time. The reality, though, is that this demand is not spread evenly throughout the network, resulting in particular problems of congestion and, for many types of transport demand, some form of **peaking** whereby demand is concentrated at particular times of the day, week or year.

- Transport demand is a **derived demand** in the sense that it derives from the needs of people (to travel to work, to go shopping or to go on holiday) and the needs of businesses (to move goods and industrial materials). The function of transport, therefore, is to provide for the satisfaction of some other need.

These features are illustrated simply in Figure 1, which shows an adaptation of the circular flow of income.

The satisfaction of transport demand is met by various **transport modes,** such as roads, railways, aeroplanes, inland waterways and so on. Table 1 provides a brief analysis of the characteristics of the main modes that are used for carrying passengers and freight.

Although transport is used as a generic term throughout this book, an understanding of the modes and their characteristics is important. It particularly helps to explain the trends in transport demand that are

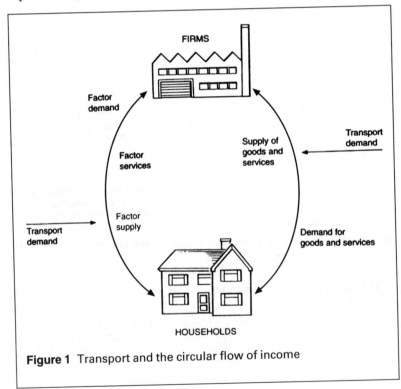

Figure 1 Transport and the circular flow of income

Split into ADV & DISADV. (handwritten annotation)

Table 1 Characteristics of the main modes of transport

Mode	Passengers	Freight
Rail	Potentially high speed over journeys of about 50–300 miles; can carry large volumes of passengers into city centres; environmentally acceptable	Bulk carrier, particularly over short distances; energy efficient; problems of interchange with road; likely to be more widely used in the future
Road	*Private car* is the most flexible and convenient of all transport modes; door to door service; comfortable and easily used for carriage of luggage, shopping etc.; *Buses* make the most efficient use of road space particularly in urban areas; main weaknesses relate to quality of service, reliability and comfort, relative to the car	Door to door service, highly used for 'just-in-time' deliveries; few transhipment problems, flexible, convenient and able to provide a high level of customer service; environmentally suspect and poor public image
Inland waterways	Some use for leisure and tourism purposes	Irrelevant in the UK but widely used for bulk carriage in other EU countries; relatively cheap but slow and inflexible compared with road and rail
Air	Speed is main strength, particularly over long distances; attractive for business and tourism; problem of intrinsic noise for those living on the flight paths	Very expensive; small carrying capacity but of obvious relevance where goods are of high value, perishable or urgent
Sea	Often the only possibility for certain types of trip; expensive on a mile for mile basis compared with other modes	Vast quantities can be moved; particular value for transport of containers over long distances
Pipelines		Well established for oil, bulk liquids, fuel and power; environmentally sound for inland use; a natural monopoly but subject to contestability

analysed in the next section, and many of the specific problems discussed in other chapters.

Transport demand in the UK

The demand for transport, of both passengers and goods, has been growing steadily over the past 45 years in the UK. In particular, road transport is now dominant. There was a particular acceleration in total demand during the 1980s with a lesser growth in demand during the 1990s.

Figures 2 and 3 show the trend in the demand for transport in Great Britain from 1981 to 1996. The compound units used in each of these figures are indicative of the nature of transport; i.e. they measure demand in terms of both volume and distance for each of the main modes of passenger and goods transport.

More particularly, Figure 2 shows the following:

- Private cars were used for 86 per cent of all passenger transport demand in 1997.
- 94 per cent of demand is for road transport. Bus and coach transport, motor cycle and pedal cycle demand are added to that of transport by cars and vans to arrive at this figure.
- The use of rail has remained relatively stable since 1991, although its market share has fallen to 5 per cent of total demand in 1996.
- The decline in use of buses and coaches has persisted, both absolutely and relatively over this period.

Correspondingly, Figure 3 shows the following:

- The total demand for goods transport has increased over the period, although recession from 1989 largely accounted for a fall in

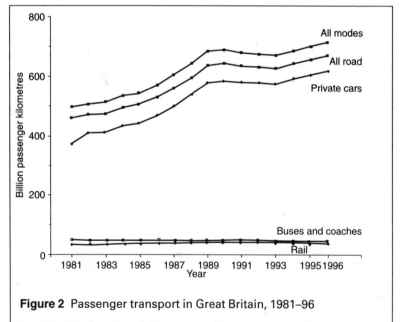

Figure 2 Passenger transport in Great Britain, 1981–96

Source: *Transport Statistics Great Britain,* Department of Transport, 1997

demand to 1992. By 1995, the 1989 all-modes level had been exceeded as the economy strengthened.

- Roads carried 66 per cent of all demand in 1996. If coastal shipping is excluded, roads had around 89 per cent of the inland market.
- The demand for transporting goods by rail has fallen over this period. Rail freight now carries just 6 per cent of all goods moved in Great Britain, 8 per cent of the inland market. Future growth prospects are good.

Trends in transport demand since the mid-1980s are particularly relevant (see Table 2). They show a pronounced increase in the demand for road transport, for both passengers and goods. The implications of the trends shown in Figures 2 and 3 and in Table 2 are far-reaching for the future. Their recognition and understanding are important as they go some way to explaining the serious problems of traffic congestion being experienced on the UK's road network (see Chapter 6) and the need for a more sustainable future transport policy (see Chapter 7).

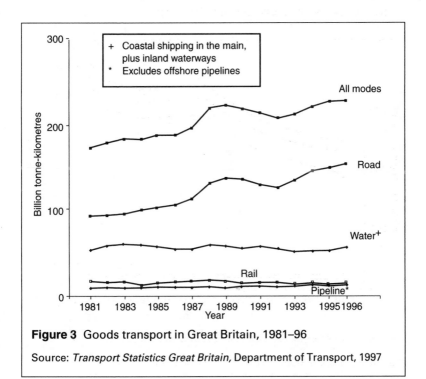

Figure 3 Goods transport in Great Britain, 1981–96

Source: *Transport Statistics Great Britain,* Department of Transport, 1997

Table 2 Transport trends in Great Britain since 1985

	Passenger transport (billion passenger-km)			Goods transport (billion tonne-km)	
	Cars and taxis	Buses and coaches	Rail	Road	Rail
1985	441	49	37	103.2	15.3
1986	465	47	37	105.4	16.6
1987	500	47	40	113.3	17.3
1988	536	46	41	130.2	18.2
1989	581	47	40	137.8	17.3
1990	588	46	40	136.3	15.8
1991	584	44	38	130.0	15.3
1992	581	43	38	126.5	15.5
1993	584	44	37	134.5	13.8
1994	595	44	35	143.7	13.0
1995	606	44	37	149.6	13.3
1996	620	44	38	153.9	na

Transport economics

The study of transport is now a recognized branch of economics. As the remainder of this book will show, many of the problems analysed and discussed by present-day transport economists can be seen as involving problems of **resource allocation**. Chapters 3–5 will consider some of these, including:

- how to allocate traffic, both passengers and goods, between the various transport modes, in particular between road and rail transport;
- how to achieve the best allocation of public expenditure in transport;
- how to achieve the right balance between the private and the public sectors, in infrastructure provision especially;
- how best to meet the needs of users of transport while at the same time safeguarding the quality of the environment.

By looking at the functions of transport this introductory chapter has confirmed Rudyard Kipling's assertion that *transport is civilization*. Transport has an essential contribution to make to 'the industrial process' and to economic well-being in general. Through its ever-increasing use, the car is a need for most families, although whether this will be true to the same extent in the future is more problematic. The remaining chapters build upon this foundation and provide a more detailed perspective of the main resource allocation problems and issues in transport.

> **KEY WORDS**
>
> Infrastructure   Transport modes
> Peaking   Resource allocation
> Derived demand

Essay topic

(a) With the aid of examples, explain why the demand for transport services is a derived demand.   [8 marks]

(b) There are several means by which a government can control the supply of transport services. Explain and comment upon their use in the UK.   [12 marks]

[University of Cambridge Local Examinations Syndicate 1996]

Data response question

Passenger transport in Great Britain: trends to 1990 and forecasts to 2025

This task is based on a question set by the University of Cambridge Local Examinations Syndicate in 1995. Study the graph in Figure A on passenger transport in Great Britain 1952–1990, and the forecast of traffic growth to 2025 (Table A), and then answer the questions. Note that 'rail' in Figure A includes British Rail, London Underground and other systems.

Table A Forecast percentage increase in vehicle use, 1988–2025

	Low estimate	High estimate
Private cars	82	134
Light goods vehicles	101	215
Heavy goods vehicles	67	141
Buses and coaches	0	0
All traffic	83	142

Source: *Roads for Prosperity,* Department of Transport, 1989

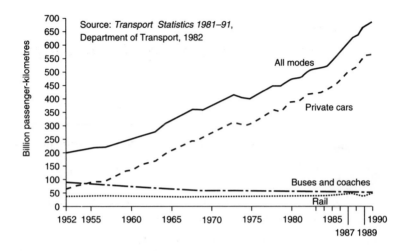

Figure A Passenger transport in Great Britain, 1952–1990

1. (a) Which mode of transport experienced the greatest fall in its share of the passenger transport market from 1952 to 1990? [1 mark]

(b) How is demand for this mode of transport expected to change over the next 30 years or so? [1 mark]

(c) State *one* time period before 1990 when the demand for passenger transport *fell* and give *two* reasons why this fall might have occurred. [3 marks]

2. The demand for passenger transport is a derived demand. State what this means and explain how it might be applied to account for the increase in transport demand from 1985. [3 marks]

3. (a) What evidence is there that traffic forecasting is inexact? [2 marks]

(b) State and explain *two* factors which are likely to determine private car traffic forecasts. [4 marks]

4. Comment on the ways in which economists might make use of these traffic forecasts. [6 marks]

Chapter Two

The economic importance of transport

'Transport links play an important role in the competitiveness of British business.' Freight Transport Association, 1997

As Figures 2 and 3 indicated, the importance of transport activity can be shown crudely by the total demand for passenger and goods transport. In addition there are various other ways in which transport's economic importance can be analysed, including:

- employment in transport operations and related activities
- current and capital expenditure by consumers, households and the government.

Some of the statistics most widely used by economists are outlined in this chapter. Over the past few years, the range and quality of transport information has increased – students who wish to develop a wider awareness should consult *Transport Statistics – Great Britain* (Stationery Office, annual) and other government publications.

Employment in transport

Transport is a substantial employer of labour in the UK economy. In 1997, for example, total transport employment was almost 1.8 million, or about one in twelve of the working population (see Table 3). About half of the total employment was in transport operations – that is, in the provision of road, rail, sea and air transport services for passengers and goods.

Over the last twenty to thirty years, total employment in transport operations has fallen. This may seem surprising in view of the continued growth in demand, but it is a reflection of:

- the long-term decline of certain modes of transport – rail, bus and sea transport especially
- the related switch from public to private passenger transport
- the massive job losses that have come about in rail transport, alongside substantial improvements in labour productivity
- the increased efficiency of all modes of transport, through technological advances and improved transport vehicles and as a consequence of privatization.

Table 3 Employment in transport, 1982–97 (in thousands)

	1982	1987	1992	1997
Transport operations				
Railways	166.5	138.8	134.4	92.5
Other inland transport	405.1	382.7	388.7	364.3
(road freight, road passenger and urban railways)				
Water transport	55.2	33.3	31.0	29.3
Air transport	46.2	53.5	60.9	58.1
Cargo handling and supporting services to transport	216.7	208.9	218.8	229.6
Travel agents and tour operators	46.1	58.3	71.0	86.0
Totals	925.8	826.8	895.0	859.7
Employment in transport-related industries				
Motor vehicle production and parts	309.4	261.5	231.8	206.8
Other transport equipment	335.2	244.1	187.0	156.8
Retail distribution	248.5	235.0	264.3	356.1
Other	177.6	184.6	199.5	171.6
Totals	1070.7	925.2	882.6	891.3
All transport industries and services	1996.5	1788.5	1767.2	1751.0

Source: Adapted from *Transport Statistics* (various)

Employment in **transport-related industries** is shown in the lower part of Table 3. Here, transport's economic importance as both a secondary and a tertiary activity is recognized. The decrease in employment in vehicle production has been particularly severe – *it is a very good example of an industry whose fortunes have suffered as a consequence of deindustrialization.* Production has been transferred to countries with lower costs. The switch to imported vehicles by many private and industrial transport users has further exaggerated the fall in output and employment.

Expenditure on transport

Transport, like any form of economic activity, contributes to the national output of the UK economy. It is, though, a difficult task to estimate this contribution because transport is a part of the recorded output of many industries – retailing, construction, communications and so on. Overall, transport accounts for around 15 per cent of GNP at factor cost, which is slightly higher than in most other EU countries. In general, as national income has risen so too has the amount spent on transport. This expenditure is made by consumers and industry.

Table 4 Index of road haulage activity and broad economic growth in Great Britain (1980 = 100)

	GDP	Manufacturing output	Construction output	Freight moved	Freight lifted	Average length of haul
1980	100	100	100	100	100	100
1981	99	94	92	101	93	108
1982	101	94	100	102	99	102
1983	104	96	106	103	97	106
1984	106	99	111	108	100	108
1985	111	102	111	110	104	106
1986	115	103	116	113	105	107
1987	121	108	129	121	110	110
1988	126	116	141	139	126	111
1989	129	121	149	147	129	114
1990	130	121	152	146	125	117
1991	127	114	140	139	114	122
1992	127	114	134	135	111	122
1993	129	115	133	143	116	124
1994	135	120	138	154	121	127
1995	138	123	137	160	122	131
1996	141	123	137	164	124	132
Percentage change:						
1980–96	41	23	37	64	24	31
1985–96	23	19	19	45	17	24
1990–96	12	9	3	21	11	9
1994–96	2	0	1	2	1	1

Source: *Economic Trends* and Reference table 3 (1986–96 only)

Figure 4 and Table 4 show that since 1987, the rate of increase of demand for road freight transport has increased at a faster rate than the growth of GDP. In contrast, the rate of growth in manufacturing output has been consistently below that of GDP growth (indicative of deindustrialization), and in recent years the rate of growth of output from construction has lagged behind that of road freight transport. It is also interesting to note that the average length of haul has increased steadily and consistently since 1980.

Table 5 shows weekly household expenditure on transport and travel from 1982 to 1996. Over this period, as a percentage of *all* **household expenditure**, the amount spent on transport and travel remained more or less steady at around 15 per cent. Within this, though, the absolute amount and proportion of total expenditure spent on the purchase and running of private cars has increased very rapidly. This is in line with the trends identified in Figure 2.

It is also interesting to observe that there has been an increase in

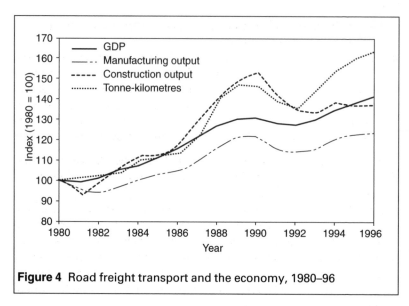

Figure 4 Road freight transport and the economy, 1980–96

household expenditure in real terms of over 20 per cent for the period to 1991, with a fall on this basis since then. The *Family Expenditure Survey* also shows two further interesting points:

• The percentage of household expenditure spent on transport and travel increases as household income increases. *There is a high, positive income elasticity of demand,* so sales expand when incomes are increasing. Conversely – as shown by declining car sales and fewer

Table 5 Household expenditure on transport and travel, 1982–96 (£ per week)

	1982	*1987*	*1991*	*1996*
Net purchase of motor vehicles	6.88	11.68	17.08	15.25
Maintenance and running of motor vehicles	9.26	12.12	17.04	21.74
Railway and tube fares	0.78	0.89	0.96	1.28
Bus and coach fares	1.20	1.14	1.25	1.25
Other	1.67	2.57	3.37	3.64
All transport and travel	19.79	28.40	39.70	43.16
Motoring expenditure as % of total	81.5	83.8	85.9	85.7
Percentage of household expenditure	14.8	15.1	15.3	14.9

Source: Adapted from *Family Expenditure Survey,* Stationery Office, 1996

foreign holidays being bought – when the economy moves into recession then sales tend to decline.

- Railways and private cars are used primarily by households in the higher income groups; in contrast, bus transport is used disproportionately by the lower income groups. *The demand for bus travel therefore has a low income elasticity of demand* – whether it is an inferior good is not an easy question to answer because it depends on complex factors relating to an individual's travel needs.

Transport is an important part of **public expenditure,** the total money spent by central and local governments on the provision of various goods and services in the UK.

Annually, transport expenditure accounts for 7–8 per cent of the total. This money is expended by central and local governments on both **capital** and **current expenditure.** The former covers major items of transport expenditure spread over various years, whereas the latter relates to items such as annual maintenance costs and **revenue support** (fares subsidies). The largest sums go into the national and local road systems (see also Chapter 4).

It is interesting to see from Table 6 that, for transport in London and by rail, grants and subsidies paid have increased in recent years, contrary to popular belief. Significantly, that paid to support local bus services outside London has fallen.

Equally pertinent has been the continued expenditure on the **Public Service Obligation** paid to the railways. This money is the government's contract with train operators to safeguard certain unremunerative passenger services outside the metropolitan areas, where the

Table 6 Expenditure on transport subsidies and grants, 1982–96 (£million)

	1982	1987	1992	1996
Rail:				
Public Service Obligation	831	775	1165	1669
Other grants, incl. from PTEs	171	171	107	362
London Transport	385	343	786	1069
Bus and tram services:				
revenue support	358	229	240	226
other, incl. concessionary fares	291	371	466	523
Total grants and subsidies, including those above	3447	2553	2676	4011

Source: Adapted from *Transport Statistics Great Britain* (various)

Passenger Transport Executives (PTEs) have this particular responsibility. The £1165 million paid in 1992 contrasted with just £473 million in 1988. Rail's financial fortunes have undoubtedly been affected by recession, as the widening gap between income and expenditure would indicate. In 1996, the sum was inflated by payments made to the new private franchise operators (see Chapter 5).

As J. M. Thomson once stated, transport 'requires capital equipment, materials and labour'. Moreover, it is an important source of private and public sector expenditure on both infrastructure and transport operations. Transport growth is therefore inextricably linked to personal and business well-being and has an important role in the competitiveness of British business.

KEY WORDS

Transport-related industries	Capital expenditure
Household expenditure	Current expenditure
Public expenditure	Revenue support
	Public Service Obligation

Essay topic

Explain the criteria that an economist would use to analyse the importance of transport in the UK economy.

Data response question

Passenger transport in the UK

This task is based on a question set by the London Examinations division of EdExcel in 1997. Study Figures A–D and Table A relating to transport, and then answer the questions that follow.

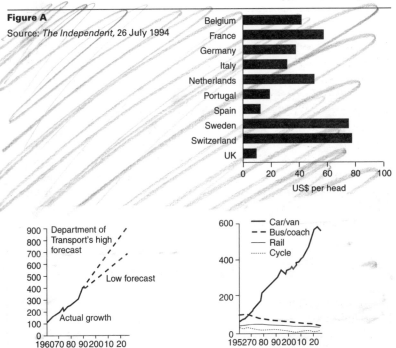

Figure A

Source: *The Independent*, 26 July 1994

Figure B UK road traffic growth (billion vehicle-km per year)

Source: *The Independent*, 27 October 1994

Figure C UK passenger transport (billion passenger-km per year)

Source: *The Independent*, 27 October 1994

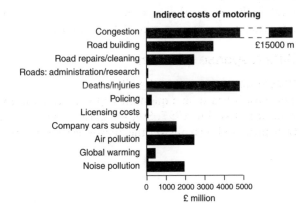

Indirect costs of motoring

£15000 m

£ million

Revenue from road users

£10700 m

£ million

Figure D UK road transport costs and revenue, 1993

Source: *The Independent*, 26 July 1994

Table A Passenger transport price indices in the UK

	1981	1986	1991	1994	1995
Fares and other travel costs	100	135	186	219	n/a
Bus and coach fares	100	139	198	242	252
Rail fares	100	137	201	241	246
Other	100	107	136	155	157
Motoring costs	100	131	163	196	n/a
Purchase of vehicles	100	116	144	158	161
Maintenance of vehicles	100	138	195	239	242
Petrol and oil	100	145	156	191	202
Vehicle tax and insurance	100	146	220	320	320
Retail price index (all items)	100	137	185	201	208

Source: *Social Trends*, HMSO, 1996

1. (a) With reference to the data, how might the changing pattern of transport use in the UK be explained? [8 marks]
   (b) What other information would you find useful in explaining these changes? [4 marks]
2. (a) With reference to Figure D, how does the use of private cars give rise to external costs? [4 marks]
   (b) To what extent do the taxes levied on road users compensate for the external costs of motoring? [3 marks]
3. Examine *one* policy which might be used to reduce the growth of road traffic in the next 20 years. [6 marks]

Chapter Three

Transport costs and pricing

*'The private car liberates but it also destroys ... We are nourishing at
immense cost a monster of great potential destructiveness ... and yet
we love him dearly!'* Sir Colin Buchanan, 1963

The nature of transport costs

Economists recognize three types of costs, which have particular relevance to transport. These are:

- **Private costs** – the opportunity costs to the individual or firm of resources used. These are based on the market value of factors purchased and include the direct operating cost paid in running various types of transport vehicle.
- **External costs** – the spillover effects which can occur if private costs and social costs are not equal. A feature of most transport operations is that these costs do occur and are *negative.*
- **Social costs** – the opportunity costs to the whole of society of the resources an individual or firm uses. In other words, these are the total costs of transport use.

Figure 5 illustrates the idea that if market demand and supply correctly reflect the marginal benefits of consumption and the marginal cost of production of a good, then there will be an efficient allocation of resources at P_o and Q_o. Here, the price at which the goods are sold equals the marginal cost of producing them; that is $P = MC$. The marginal social cost (MSC) of providing a commodity or service equals the marginal social benefit (MSB) derived from its consumption.

This optimum does not occur in most transport markets, where the private costs and benefits fail to reflect adequately the costs and benefits to society of providing the services concerned. External costs in the form of traffic congestion, noise pollution, exhaust emissions and so on do occur, with marginal social cost greater than marginal private cost. Consequently, *there is a misallocation of resources* as the MSB and MSC curves differ from the market demand and supply curves. Moreover, there is a powerful case for government intervention in such markets to improve the allocation of resources (see below).

Private costs, as shown in Table 7, can be subdivided into three main elements, namely:

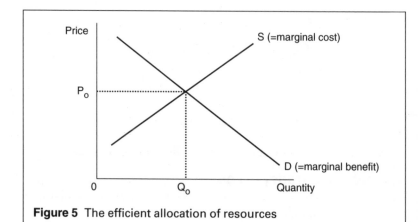

Figure 5 The efficient allocation of resources

Table 7 Cost structure of main modes of transport operations

Mode	Fixed costs	Variable costs	Other*
Private cars	Capital costs, insurance, road tax, depreciation	Fuel, maintenance, tyres	–
Heavy goods vehicles	Capital costs, licences, insurance, depreciation	Fuel, maintenance, tyres, drivers' wages	Terminal costs
Rail	Track costs, administrative and overhead charges	Fuel, maintenance, labour costs	Terminal costs (freight)
Air	Capital costs, administrative and overhead charges	Fuel, maintenance, landing charges, in-flight services, labour costs	
Sea	Capital costs, insurance, administrative and overhead charges	Fuel, maintenance, in-voyage costs, harbour costs	

*Terminals for rail passengers, air and sea transport are now usually owned by organizations other than operators

- **Fixed costs** – these in general consist of the costs of making transport vehicles available for use. Rail is unusual in so far as, at present, track costs are included.
- **Variable costs** – these directly depend on the way in which transport vehicles are used and the level of service that is available.
- Terminal costs – these apply to some modes and in most cases can be included in fixed costs.

This distinction is important. In railway operation, for example, fixed costs are a relatively high proportion of total costs. Once a stretch of railway track is open for use, the average cost per train falls as the number of trains using the line increases.

Table 8 shows a cost breakdown in these terms for two sizes of heavy goods vehicle. It introduces a further cost concept, that of **semi-fixed costs** – that is, costs that are not entirely dependent on the use made of vehicles. In this case, firms normally have a core staff of drivers to pay, even though they may not always be fully employed in working with the vehicles. This table also illustrates how firms can benefit from **economies of scale** – a reduction in long-run average costs – through the use of heavier goods vehicles. The average cost per tonne of pay-load of 38-tonne vehicle operation is 8.6 per cent less than that of operating 32-ton vehicles, the legal permitted maximum until May 1983. This particular benefit is a very powerful one used by industry to support their argument for 40/44-tonne operations.

An additional benefit of larger vehicles is that fewer vehicles would be needed to move a given tonnage of goods. In turn, this would mean

Table 8 Annual costs of operating 32-ton and 38-tonne articulated goods vehicles*

	32-ton gvw (£)	38 tonne gvw (£)
Fixed costs		
Finance costs	3 350	3 800
Licences	2 450	3 100
Insurances	200	200
Depreciation	4 400	5 000
Semi-fixed costs		
Drivers' wages	10 800	11 500
Variable costs		
Fuel	9 220	9 725
Tyres	1 700	2 500
Maintenance	7 500	8 500
Total costs	**39 620**	**44 325**
Typical payload	20 tonnes	24.5 tonnes
Cost per year per tonne of payload	1 981	1 810

*Based on 50 000 miles a year and finance costs of 10% p.a. on capital cost of vehicle
Source: Freight Transport Association, 1985

fewer vehicles on the roads, reduced congestion, fuel savings and certain environmental benefits. The downside, though, is that it would make it more difficult for the railways to gain new freight business. Recognizing these conflicts, in 1997 the government announced that from January 1999 the maximum permitted weight of goods vehicle would be increased to 40 tonnes, for five-axle combinations. The 44 tonne maximum applies only where vehicles are carrying containers and swap-bodies to and from rail terminals.

A further application of these cost concepts is in passenger transport, where 'load factors' are an important consideration. This term refers to the proportion of space or seats offered for sale which is actually paid for and taken up by fare-paying passengers. Perhaps the best illustration is in air transport where fixed costs are a high proportion of total costs. Because of this, very lucrative last-minute deals are often provided by tour operators for people looking for a cheap holiday! Variable costs have to be covered but the price paid is also likely to make a contribution to fixed costs.

The external costs of transport

Transport, of course, contributes to the environmental problems that face us. There is little argument that transport pollutes the environment and, through CO_2 emissions, it is a major contributor to the greenhouse effect and global warming. Within transport it is the road sector that attracts most criticism and cause for concern. Other modes, particularly rail, are more environmentally friendly for the carriage of passengers and freight than road transport.

At a more local level, transport imposes much more localized external costs, particularly on those living and working in urban areas close to main roads, transport depots and so on. These **negative externalities** include:

- *Noise.* Lorries in particular cause high levels of disturbance. Traffic noise produces a level of pitch which over long periods becomes unwelcome to the human ear. Prolonged exposure to traffic noise can disrupt lifestyle, increase stress and make it difficult to relax.
- *Pollution.* Road traffic produces gaseous emissions, particularly from exhaust systems. As with noise, the local incidence of pollution from lorries is greater than that from cars. Diesel engines are rather 'greener' than their petrol equivalents, although there is particular concern over nitrous oxide emissions.
- *Visual intrusion.* This is a less obvious negative externality and relates to situations where road traffic impairs or devalues the view in an

'Smash the next lamp on the left, flatten the pavement by the pub, nudge the sweetshop, scrape the Market Cross, then just follow the skidmarks to London.'

urban or rural landscape. Sadly, in many historic cities, buildings seem to rise from a plinth of cars and visitors and residents obtain less visual enjoyment than they might from their surroundings.

- *Blight.* Again, urban road transport is the main culprit. This type of negative externality is invariably caused by planning and similar problems associated with the building of new roads or providing facilities to speed up the traffic flow.
- *Accidents.* Road traffic accidents are very costly to the community, in terms of the physical damage caused and in the serious injuries and loss of life which can occur.

The above are in addition to further negative externalities as a consequence of traffic congestion (see Chapter 6).

These problems were recognized by the Royal Commission on Environmental Pollution (RCEP) in 1971 when it produced its first report. In 1994 and in 1997, the Commission has published highly critical and controversial reports, in which it has proposed a fundamental shift and complete rethink on transport policy. Details of their proposals are contained in Chapter 7. The boxed item on page 25 shows their estimates for these negative externalities.

Underlying the recommendations is the fact that, at present, owing to **negative externalities,** the price paid by the transport users is lower and the quantity demanded is greater than the **social optimum** at which price

The slow road to hypocrisy

LORD HANSON

To own a car has been a lifelong dream for most of us and an unmatched blessing. Its speed, reliability and ready availability, undreamed of in the past, give us a mobility and freedom now taken for granted.

The car supports the breadwinner's job and improves family life and leisure in ways that not even the most comprehensive system of public transport could ever provide. But this great personal boon is now under threat.

Many a motorist will be asking if there is no one in the public arena prepared to speak up for the car, or in favour of building new roads. Do our lives have to be governed by "green" minorities? Is no one willing to admit doubts over the so-called merits of a Whitehall-inspired "integrated" public system?

Instead the embattled car owner is offered one daft scheme after another. The latest suggestion is to curb the use of the M5 and M6 motorways by restricting access for local drivers.

The recent government about-face on roads neatly encapsulates our double standards. The Chancellor of the Exchequer puts a swingeing increase on the existing 72 per cent tax on petrol and diesel, despite the fact that less than 30 per cent of the £23 billion taxes raised on motoring is used for road building and maintenance. It seems that motorists are being used as a milch-cow for all those other areas that the State wants to spend our money on.

John Prescott, the minister responsible, supposedly a great friend of the working – and driving – man, adds his bit with the review or cancellation of vitally-needed road improvements. In what century are these people that dream up our transport policy living?

When Prescott had to make a decision on 12 contentious road schemes, he stopped two, approved five and deferred decisions on five... Why the indecision when the argument for new roads is compelling?

Despite the cost – easily affordable from the road fund tax – better roads are essential to reduce the gridlocks that bedevil us. And we must encourage ample parking in towns. North America can give us lessons because new businesses will only open if they can be sure their customers can get to them...

When we consider road freight, in which business I spent most of my early working days, the prospect is frightening. Ninety per cent of goods go by road. No imaginable future or past railway system could, with such ease, flexibility and cheapness, bring us the fresh food and other products we need daily.

Who of us is prepared to pay for the cost and inconvenience of having essential goods delayed by rail? Not the merchants, certainly, nor especially the consumer and tax-paying voter.

Cars and lorries – the latter pay the bulk of the road and fuel taxes – are blamed for pollution, but this ignores the massive technological advances in engine design that have reduced emissions by 90 per cent in the past 20 years and will continue to make motoring even cleaner...

Of course, as car critics like to point out, there are still too many road injuries. But the number of fatalities has halved since 1966. Let us not forget that statistics show the home is a most dangerous place, yet no one suggests its abolition.

The roads solution is to find a balance between safety and some discomfort on the one hand and personal freedom of choice on the other. All the evidence is that current planned road improvements are vital to move us into the next century. They are also vital for the economic growth of the country, not forgetting the car industry and the road materials companies which will survive or fail on this.

Express on Sunday, 17 August 1997

The estimated external and social costs of road transport in Great Britain (£ billion a year, 1994 prices)

Air pollution	2.0–5.2
Climatic change	1.5–3.1
Noise and vibration	<u>1.0–4.6</u>
Total external costs	4.5–12.9
Road accidents	5.4
Social costs of road transport	9.9–18.3

Note: The estimates of external costs are very difficult to estimate with precision, hence the range of values shown. They do, though, provide a broad indication of the scale of harm caused by road transport. The costs of congestion are not included.

---

equals marginal social cost. This situation is shown in Figure 6. As things stand, there is no incentive to reduce transport demand as users do not pay the full or true cost involved. Moreover, vehicle users gain at the expense of other groups in society. The economist's answer here is to introduce an **indirect tax** (or 'green tax') to equate marginal social cost and marginal social benefit. (See also Figure 14.)

This approach is fine in theory, but in practice it is very difficult to apply, not least because there are genuine obstacles to recognizing and measuring all the social costs and benefits involved. Even so, the RCEP do clearly acknowledge that negative externalities are a serious issue and that a radical sea-change approach is needed in order to avert ever-more serious environmental problems from increased transport demand.

The track costs argument

Over the past twenty years or so, economists have debated the '**track costs**' argument, particularly in the context of road provision. In short, it involves the issue of who pays and who benefits from the way in which roads are provided.

Table 9 on page 27 shows the basis of this argument. The final column indicates that all classes of users in 1994/95 covered their track costs; that is, the construction and maintenance costs allocated to them for the use that they made of the road network. As the table shows, cars especially cover track costs by a magnitude of 3.7 to 1. Heavy goods vehicles and buses and coaches also cover their direct

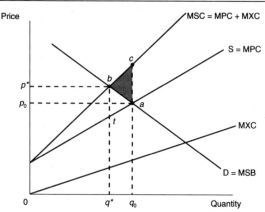

(MXC = marginal external costs; MPC = marginal private costs; MSC = marginal social costs)

Allocative efficiency is achieved where MSC = MSB.

The MSC schedule is the vertical sum of MPC and MXC.
The private market extends production to q_0, where D = S,
but for each unit between q^* and q_0, MSC is greater than MSB.
These units should not be produced.
The deadweight loss from their production is given by the shaded
triangle *abc*.

Consequently:

Social costs   >   Private costs
[Total costs of use of road space]   [Costs of use of road space to users]

Quantity demanded is higher than optimum.
Price paid by users is lower than optimum.

REMEDY: INCREASED TAXATION SO THAT MSC = MSB
(a green tax)

Figure 6 Private and social costs divergence
(adapted from *Equity, Efficiency and Market Failure* by M. Wilkinson,
Heinemann Educational, 1997)

road costs but by the smallest proportion of any class of user, 1.4:1.
The total tax paid by road users consists of various indirect taxes such
as fuel tax, car tax, vehicle excise duty, value added tax and so on.

The original idea behind the Road Fund Tax (the Vehicle Excise
Duty as it is now known) was that receipts from it were to be ploughed
back into the road network to provide for users. In other words, it was
hypothecated for road-building and on-going maintenance. This is no
longer the case. On the contrary, there are valid arguments, related to

Table 9 Projected road taxation and track costs

Class of vehicle	Total tax	Road costs	Taxes:cost ratio
Cars, light vans and taxis	14 610	3 990	3.7:1
Motorcycles	70	20	3.5:1
Buses and coaches	360	255	1.4:1
Goods vehicles below 3.5 tonnes gvw	2 740	2 030	1.4:1
Other vehicles	320	155	2.1:1
Totals	**18 110**	**6 445**	

Source: Adapted from *Transport Statistics,* Department of Transport, 1994

the cost of externalities, why private car users should pay additional taxation. Commercial vehicles, because of their production-related use of roads, should similarly only be taxed to cover their direct road costs. The information in Table 9 can therefore be used to argue for:

- less taxes to be paid by commercial vehicle users and buses and coaches
- even higher taxes for private car users.

THE TRANSPORT DILEMMA

The Freight Transport Association believes that the demand for freight transport will continue to increase over the next 20 years, probably above government forecasts. At the same time, congestion will get worse.

All road users must share the responsibility for making best use of transport resources. There must be an on-going commitment to a package of measures leading to the maximum investment in transport infrastructure. Cars are and always will be the main problem – the whole population must make a determined effort to curb the use of cars and promote a greater use of and commitment to public transport. This will allow road freight vehicles to move around more efficiently.

The ultimate aim must be one of hypothecation of infrastructure funds from road user revenues. There must be an irrevocable commitment to a new roads programme and a minimum standard created for access to ports, cities, industrial and urban areas.

Source: Adapted from *Transport Dilemma: Caring for Society's Freight Transport Needs Over the Next 20 Years,* Freight Transport Association, 1991

This view, indeed, is one that has been promoted for some time by the Freight Transport Association, the leading user trade association in freight transport in the UK. The boxed item on the previous page shows a summary of their 'Transport Dilemma' arguments.

Notwithstanding this, looking ahead, future taxation policy is most likely to continue the trend of increasing the level of taxation on private road users as this goes some way to meeting the very strong environmental arguments raised in the previous section for cutting back on private car use and using vehicles much more efficiently than at present.

Price discrimination

Within a broadly defined market, different market segments are likely to have different price elasticities of demand. In such circumstances, the theory behind **price discrimination** is that *total revenue will be maximized if marginal revenues are equalized across all market segments*, in order to determine the quantities to be offered in each segment. Prices are then set in accordance with the price elasticity of demand in each segment. The more inelastic the demand, the higher the price. In the extreme cases, each customer would be treated individually and be charged a price which reduced his or her **consumer surplus** to zero and thus maximized total revenue for the producer.

In practice, perfect price discrimination as described above is not possible. Appropriate market segments therefore need to be price identified, and estimates made of the price elasticity of demand in each case. Pricing systems then must be developed, that not only raise prices in the less elastic market segments, but also prevent those customers from trading down to the cheaper segments.

The UK rail passenger market has experienced this form of pricing since the early 1970s, particularly for longer distance and intercity tickets. On routes to London the business travel segment is particularly significant, and competition from other modes, including the private car, is relatively weak. *Price elasticities are estimated at less than unity*, particularly for arrival in London in time for morning business meetings. Thus tickets for such journeys command the highest prices.

In the leisure and social travel markets, including visiting friends and relatives, competition from other modes such as express coaches is stronger, and the precise time of travel is less important. *Price elasticities of demand in these market segments are greater than unity*. Much lower fares are offered to extract revenue through increased volumes of business in these segments, but availability of these cheaper tickets is restricted to minimize their use by business travellers.

In the market segments most sensitive to price (where competition from other modes is strongest and where customers may be less well off and are likely to be disuaded from travel altogether), further discounts are given. These are frequently given via railcards such as the Family Railcard, the Senior Citizens Card and the Young Persons Card, because once again these schemes promote increased volumes of traffic but minimize the loss of revenue from segments such as business travel where price elasticities are significantly lower.

Price differentials between market segments are often substantial because of the significant variations in demand elasticities. This point is clearly shown in Table 10, which demonstates the wide range of fares available for rail travellers between Leeds and London.

Table 10 Standard Class rail fares between Leeds and King's Cross (London) in November 1997

Open Return	£102	This ticket is aimed at the business travel market and is completely unrestricted
Saver Return	£58	This fare offers a huge reduction on the Open Return but cannot be used for arrival in London before 11.00 a.m.
Supersaver	£48	This ticket offers a further significant saving but cannot be used on Fridays. Return from London on peak early evening services is not allowed. Not valid for travel before 10.00
Superadvance	£38	This ticket circumvents the restrictions on the Supersaver ticket but must be booked at least one day in advance. Numbers are restricted on busy trains. Precise choice of train for both directions must be made at time of booking
Apex	£28	Apex tickets must be booked at least one week in advance. Numbers are restricted on busy trains, and the precise choice of train for both directions must be made at the time of booking, effectively reducing their value for business travel
Daypex	£19	This is a short-term promotional version of the Apex ticket, and is specifically for travel at weekends when business travel is much less significant. Advance booking is essential

Transport subsidy and its effects on pricing

On many passenger transport services, there is little prospect that fares can be set at levels which will generate large volumes of business and provide a commercial rate of return to the operator. Many urban, sub-urban and rural bus and rail services fall into this category. (See also Chapter 5.)

In principle, the availability of **subsidies** or revenue support can help to reduce the prices paid by passengers, and to boost patronage on the services concerned. This will generate a range of social benefits such as reduced traffic congestion and enhanced mobility for the less well off.

As shown by Figure 7, the receipt of subsidy by transport operators acts to shift the supply curve down and to the right, so that any selected output can be offered to the public at a reduced price. Intersection with the downward-sloping demand curve re-establishes market equilibrium with the quantity increased to Q_2 and the price reduced to P_2.

In practice, however, the use of subsidies to fund fare reductions is not widespread in the UK and has been decreasing in real terms. Subsidies to bus operators to maintain fares at low levels are relatively uncommon outside larger urban areas. Many rural local authorities provide subsidies only to pay for fare reductions to identified groups in need, such as pensioners and the disabled. Subsidies on unprofitable rural rail routes simply cover the notional shortfall in the costs of oper-

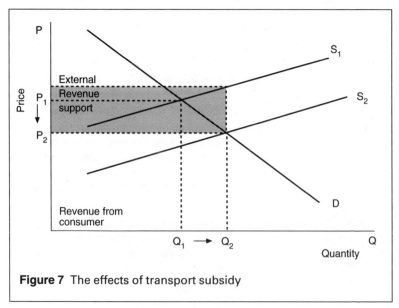

Figure 7 The effects of transport subsidy

ating such routes, and fares reflect the national level of rail fares rather than the level of subsidy received.

It is in the main conurbations, and particularly the metropolitan areas, *where local subsidies for bus and rail services are reflected in the prices charged to the general traveller.* In some regions the fares reduction due to the level of subsidy can be quite significant.

In England, the following trends in central and local government expenditure on transport subsidies can be identified since 1991/92:

- Expenditure on concessionary fares for senior citizens and young people has increased slightly to £436 million in 1996/97.
- Revenue support for local bus services fell until 1995/96; thereafter there has been a slight rise back to the 1991/92 level of £220 million.
- Revenue support for rail services in metropolitan areas outside London has increased significantly, owing to the continued committment by Passenger Transport Executives to local rail network development. In 1996/97 this stood at £200 million, twice its 1991/92 level.
- All subsidies and grants for transport in London have increased to 1996/97, except for revenue support which is now internally funded by London Transport with no direct government help.

The main argument for subsidizing passenger transport, therefore, is one of **social equity**. Transport is provided at a subsidized fare and, in some cases, certain groups in the community who cannot afford to pay the full market price receive particular benefit or support for cheaper travel. There are other arguments to support subsidies being paid to passenger transport. These include the following:

- *Where public transport, such as in large towns and cities, generates* **positive externalities.** Urban bus and rail services, for example, make a much better use of roadspace than private cars, and an efficient passenger transport system can help to reduce the effects of traffic congestion.
- *Where new transport facilities may help in* **urban regeneration,** *such as in the case of new rapid transit systems like the Manchester Metrolink and Sheffield Supertram projects.* In such cases, a new Light Rail Transit system may help to attract new businesses and create jobs to previously run-down parts of the city.
- *Where it is desirable to encourage the use of public transport for environmental reasons,* such as with a park and ride system in an historic city such as Cambridge or York.

Not all economists agree with these arguments. There are other views as to why the level of subsidy should be reduced. These include:

- The blanket nature of subsidy means that it is difficult to direct subsidy to those who really need it. Perhaps the best example of this is rail commuter fares, where all travellers, regardless of income, pay the same fares.
- The view that subsidy breeds inefficiency. It is invariably the case that the costs of public sector transport operators are higher than those in the private sector; consequently operating costs are higher than they need be.
- The idea that managers of subsidized businesses lack motivation to keep costs down, and so reduce the drain on the public purse.

These latter arguments have had a significant bearing on transport policy towards local bus services and the railways (see Chapter 5). The government is not against subsidy as such – what it does require, though, is that, where a subsidy is paid, then the receipt of public money should make its recipients more accountable.

In retrospect, much of what Sir Colin Buchanan had to say about the problems of traffic in towns has been shown to be correct. It is a matter of some regret that a generation of transport planners, who have seemingly been implementing his ideas, have not paid more attention to the man who saw it all coming. For Lord Hanson, though, the preservation of the personal freedom which only the car can provide is an overriding consideration.

KEY WORDS

Private costs	Indirect tax
External costs	Allocative efficiency
Social costs	Track costs
Fixed costs	Hypothecation
Variable costs	Price discrimination
Semi-fixed costs	Consumer surplus
Economies of scale	Subsidies
Load factors	Social equity
Negative externalities	Positive externalities
Social optimum	Urban regeneration

Reading list
Wilkinson, M., Chapter 5 in *Equity, Efficiency and Market Failure,* 2nd edn, Heinemann Educational, 1997.

Essay topics
1. 'Everyone expects to be able to drive their cars and have endless supplies of pure water from their taps but equally they expect to walk in the countryside and enjoy wildlife. Everyone would like the reservoir or motorway to be built somewhere other than where they are.' (J. Wales, *Investigating Social Issues*)
   (a) Explain the following economic terms: (i) opportunity cost; (ii) externalities; (iii) Pareto optimality. [12 marks]
   (b) Apply these concepts to the welfare economic issues contained in the above statement. [13 marks]
   [University of Cambridge Local Examinations Syndicate 1994]
2. (a) Describe the main negative externalities associated with the increased use of private cars in urban areas. [8 marks]
   (b) Discuss, in theory and in practice, how the costs of such negative externalities might be paid for for by motorists. [12 marks]
   [University of Cambridge Local Examinations Syndicate 1996]
3. (a) Explain the difference between subsidy and cross-subsidization when applied to transport. [8 marks]
   (b) Assess the likely effects of recent government policies aimed at reducing subsidy and removing cross-subsidization in the transport sector. [12 marks]
   [University of Cambridge Local Examinations Syndicate, specimen paper, 1994]
4. To what extent does the increase in private car ownership in the UK constitute an economic problem? Discuss the case for subsidizing the provision of public transport in the UK.
   [Northern Examination and Assessment Board 1994]

Data response question
The economics of heavier goods vehicles (HGVs)
This task is based on a question set by the University of Cambridge Local Examinations Syndicate in 1996. Read the next paragraph and study Tables A and B. Then answer the questions that follow.

In May 1983, the maximum permitted weight of goods vehicle allowed on the road network in the UK increased from 32.5 tonnes to 38 tonnes, for articulated vehicles with five or more axles. This maximum general limit still applies, although all other EU countries except the UK have a 40 tonne limit or above. There is continued pressure for the UK to fall in line with the rest of the EU, and many industrial users for some time have been pressing for a 44 tonne limit.

Table A Goods moved in Great Britain by type of vehicle, 1983–94 (billion tonne-kilometres)

Year	Rigid vehicles	Articulated vehicles 33 tonnes or less	Over 33 tonnes	Total
1983	35.9	50.7	5.7	92.3
1984	35.9	43.2	17.5	96.6
1985	34.6	36.8	27.6	99.0
1986	34.0	33.0	34.2	101.2
1987	35.2	29.8	43.6	108.6
1988	40.5	28.9	55.4	124.8
1989	42.4	25.7	63.9	132.0
1990	40.6	21.8	68.3	130.7
1991	40.0	17.4	70.1	127.5
1992	36.2	16.7	68.4	121.3
1993	36.5	16.5	75.6	128.6
1994	38.4	16.9	82.5	137.8

Table B Typical costs of operating three types of HGV (£ per annum)

	32.5 tonnes HGV	38 tonnes HGV	44 tonnes HGV
Drivers' wages	12,509	13,135	13,634
Licences/insurance	6,710	7,159	6,240
Depreciation	8,618	11,596	3,022
Overhead costs	10,514	11,539	12,600
Fuel/oil	15,030	17,502	20,280
Tyres	3,024	3,534	3,870
Maintainance	6,504	6,696	7,200
Total operating costs	**62,909**	**71,161**	**76,857**
Typical payload	20 tonnes	24.5 tonnes	29.5 tonnes
Cost per tonne of payload	3145	2905	2605

Notes: Costs are based on 100 000 km per annum. HGV refers to gross vehicle weight (i.e. weight of vehicle and its load). Overhead costs include vehicle finance and business establishment costs

© M T Logistica, January 1995, reproduced by permission

1. (a) Use Table A to describe how the different types of vehicle to move goods in Great Britain has changed over the period 1983 to 1994. [3 marks]
2. (a) From Table B, give an example of a fixed cost and a variable cost. Explain your answer. [4 marks]
   (b) How good is the evidence that economies of scale exist in HGV operations? [4 marks]
3. State and explain how goods vehicles might affect (i) the total number of vehicles on the roads, and (ii) the efficiency with which goods are moved by road. [4 marks]
4. Assess the economic arguments for the introduction of HGVs up to 44 tonnes. [5 marks]

Chapter Four

Investment in transport

'Funding for roads has been slashed every year since 1993. The UK transport system is already in chaos and these cuts will make it worse.' Automobile Association spokesman, 1997

The nature of transport investment

Investment is the production of goods that are not for immediate consumption. In other words, *investment increases the stock of capital in an economy.* In the context of transport, there are two main types of investment decision that have to be taken; these involve the authorization of various types of transport infrastructure and the purchase of vehicles, as implied by the definition of transport in Chapter 1. Economics provides a framework for investment decisions which include:

- Should a new stretch of motorway be built?
- Should a transport business purchase another vehicle or construct a new distribution centre?
- Should a railway station be reopened?
- Should a new rapid transit system go ahead?

An increasing number of decisions in transport are taken by the private sector, using recognized methods of investment appraisal. However, many decisions are still made by the public sector, particularly with respect to transport infrastructure investment, for which private sector methods of appraisal are inappropriate as market prices do not apply. Investment on roads is a rather good example of how the government has had to develop particular procedures in order to allocate resources.

Much transport investment by the public sector is in **public goods**. These are goods which the free market would underproduce or not produce at all. Public goods have two important characteristics:

- **Non-excludability** – the provision of a good or service cannot be made to one person without it being available for others. There is, though, a problem of *free-riders* in so far as it is impossible to prevent external benefits being enjoyed by those who have not paid for the particular good or service.

- **Non-rivalry** – the consumption of a good or service by any one person does not prevent others from enjoying it.

These theoretical characteristics are shown in the following box.

CLASSIFICATION OF TRANSPORT GOODS

	EXCLUDABLE	NON-EXCLUDABLE
RIVAL	(i) Private goods	(iii) Quasi-private goods
NON-RIVAL	(iv) Quasi-public goods	(ii) Public goods

Examples:
(i)   private cars, airline tickets, airports, Channel Tunnel
(ii)   pavements, lighthouses
(iii)   cheap off-peak travel for pensioners
(iv)   roads

It is interesting to note that the provision of road space is not a pure public good. It is called a **quasi-public good** because there is some element of excludability – only drivers with current licences can legally use roads and people below the age of 17 are excluded along with other non-car-owners from directly using roads. It might also be argued that rivalry occurs through the nature of increased traffic congestion. (See Chapter 6.)

Table 11 shows investment in transport in Great Britain in 1995/96, compared with 1985/86, subdivided between infrastructure and vehicles. The purchase of cars is by far the largest item and – related to this – public sector investment on roads is the greatest infrastructure investment, having increased by 72 per cent since 1985/86. Private road investment was just £87 million in 1995/96, mainly accounted for by the Dartford – Thurrock Bridge, the Second Severn River Crossing and the Skye Road Bridge. Overall this expenditure was only a little more than 2 per cent of the expenditure made by central and local governments on road infrastructure. The resources coming from the private sector will increase in the future, particularly with the

Table 11 Transport investment in 1995/96(£million)

	Investment	% change from 1985/86
Road infrastructure		
public	4 121	+72
private	87	†
Road vehicles		
cars	22 400	+100
other	5 700	+97
National rail infrastructure	900	+93
National rail rolling stock	200	+138
Port infrastructure	165	+47
Airports infrastructure	576	+167

†There was no private sector investment in 1985/86.
Source: *Transport Statistics Great Britain,* Stationery Office, 1997

approval of the scheme for the Birmingham Northern Relief Road, the UK's first private motorway, in July 1997.

Investment in transport infrastructure is:

- long-term in nature, often appraised over a 25–50 year timescale
- expensive, involving vast sums of capital expenditure
- seen as generating various externalities, both positive and negative
- a very important form of capital expenditure by central and local governments.

These characteristics are significant because, for most transport infrastructure expenditure, no direct charge is made to the user. The best example is, of course, the case of roads, where users do not directly pay for the use they make of the network in the UK. Two fundamental questions have to be asked:

- How does the government determine expenditure on roads?
- How does it determine which roads will actually be constructed?

Over the past 30 years or so, economists have used **cost–benefit analysis** (CBA) to provide the answers to questions like these. CBA seeks to establish the overall costs and benefits to society of a particular project such as the construction of a new stretch of motorway. More specifically: *'Cost–benefit analysis is a practical way of assessing the desirability of a project where it is necessary to take a long view and a wide view.'* (Prest and Turvey)

STEP-BY-STEP PROCEDURES OF COST–BENEFIT ANALYSIS

- Identification of all costs and benefits.
- Enumeration of all costs and benefits; i.e. putting a monetary value on them.
- Assessment of risk and uncertainty in forecasting costs and benefits.
- The effects of time; discounting of costs of benefits to establish net present value.
- Recommendation, based on the calculation of rate of return on capital employed.

In taking a 'long' view, CBA recognizes the long-term nature of transport infrastructure decisions and seeks to forecast various important variables over the full length of life of a project, as well as over the very early years. In the case of roads this might be over 25–35 years.

In taking a 'wide' view, CBA seeks to take into account the side-effects of transport infrastructure investment on people, industries, regions and so on.

Some account of externalities, therefore, is built into the CBA objectives and procedures. Whether these externalities can be valued is a rather different matter. The main stages in cost–benefit analysis are shown in the box above.

Since the early 1960s these procedures have been applied to the appraisal of many major transport projects in the UK, and rather more routinely to the construction of motorways and trunk routes. The remainder of this chapter will look at some examples.

The COBA method of appraisal for roads

COBA is the method of appraisal used by the Department of Transport to evaluate new motorway and trunk road schemes. In simple terms it compares the cost of a new road project with the benefits which can be derived by road users. An outline of what is in practice a very complex process is shown in Figure 8.

Why are new roads and motorways built? The simple answer is that they are constructed in order to speed up the flow of traffic and so reduce travel times for car and lorry drivers using them. More specifically, three main types of reduction in user costs are recognized:

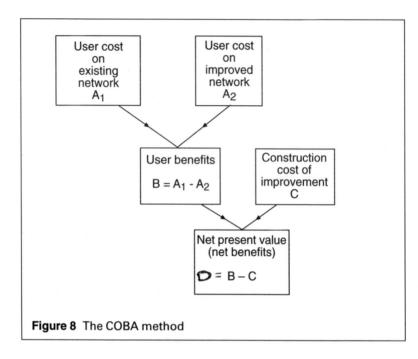

Figure 8 The COBA method

- *Journey time savings* – these are normally the most important item in the total benefits from a new road scheme. They are based on the idea that 'time is money'; in other words, the time spent in travelling has a value to the occupants of a vehicle because, if journey times are reduced, the time saved can be used to more meaningful effect. Such time savings are aggregated for all users and a monetary value put on them. This value depends on the purpose of the trip and the mode of transport for work trips – economic activity status is of relevance in determining the value of time for non-work trips.

- *Vehicle operating cost savings* – with the construction of a new stretch of road, vehicles travel not only faster but they can be used in a way which reduces fuel consumption and the wear and tear costs on the brakes, clutch and other parts of the vehicle. These cost savings may be particularly significant for commercial vehicle operators, who require fewer vehicles to do the same amount of work.

- *Accident cost savings* – new motorways and trunk roads are safer to travel on for users, mile for mile, than older roads. Consequently, the probability of experiencing an accident is reduced. The benefits from a reduction in the number and severity of accidents are given a monetary value based on a direct financial cost to individuals, their vehicles and the emergency services, the loss of output of those killed or injured and an allowance for pain, grief and suffering resulting from personal injury or death.

On the expenditure side, COBA takes into account two main costs:

- *Capital costs* – these accrue in the early years of construction of a new road and include the costs of land purchase, road construction, administrative and design costs. With new motorways costing many millions of pounds a mile, this is a major cost item.
- *Maintenance costs* – these are self-explanatory and cover the cost of street lighting, cleaning, maintenance and future resurfacing work.

As shown in Figure 8, the costs and user benefits are then compared to ascertain whether any net value can be gained from the construction of a new road scheme. Where this is so, the **net present value** (NPV) is positive, indicating that there will be some benefit to the community if the road is built. Whether a particular road is constructed, though, will depend on how the NPV in relation to its capital cost compares with other competing schemes. It will also depend on the amount of government expenditure available and the extent to which the road's construction may meet other objectives.

The COBA model has three main practical purposes:

- It establishes whether there is a *need* for a new road scheme.
- It allows *priorities* to be determined. This is normally done on the basis of a rate of return on the capital employed for its construction, also taking into account its length of life.
- It can provide the *basis for a wider discussion* at any public enquiry which may take place.

Criticisms of COBA

Owing to the scale of public expenditure involved and the persistent problem of the demand for new road schemes exceeding the funding that is available, there can be little argument that some method of appraisal is required in order for rational decisions on the construction of new roads to be taken. The cost–benefit approach laid down in COBA can, however, be criticized on various points:

- *It is a user-based method of appraisal* – it looks at whether a new road scheme is needed purely from the perspective of those car users and commercial vehicle operators who will be using it. All new roads, though, have a much wider impact, resulting in various externalities, usually negative, and which are not taken into account in the model. *It is therefore not a fully comprehensive model,* covering all who might be affected by the construction of a new road.

- Over the past 20 years or so, there has been increasing concern over the *environmental effects* of building new roads. As indicated in Table 12, these effects can be substantial and they have provided cause for concern whenever any new road scheme has been proposed. In response to such criticism the Department of Transport now incorporates an assessment of environmental suitability into various stages of the appraisal process, although no monetary value is as yet given to the *negative externalities* involved.

- Certain *value judgements* have to be made. In particular, the valuation of travel time has been the cause of much dispute – a market price is being allocated to something for which no direct charge is made by individuals.

- The **indirect effects** of constructing new roads, particularly in terms of regional development benefits, are not taken into account by the COBA model. There has been a long on-going debate about the extent to which a new road generates a positive economic impact on the area through which it passes. It has also been argued that new roads provide substantial benefits to industrial users that are not included in COBA (see next section for more details).

Government policy for roads in the 1990s

In May 1989, the government published two important Command Papers which had an important bearing on transport policy for roads in the 1990s. These policy statements announced:

- the biggest ever programme of motorway and trunk road construction

- opportunities for the private sector to fund certain new road projects, with clear implications for the way in which users pay for their use of the network.

Table 12 Environmental effects of a new road scheme

Road construction	Loss of valuable land, especially farmland. One mile of motorway needs c. 25 acres of land and 0.25 million tonnes of sand and gravel
Negative externalities	Traffic noise, visual intrusion, loss of amenity once open for use, increased atmospheric pollution. These effects can be particularly severe for those living close to a new road scheme

The main purpose of the *Roads for Prosperity* programme was to reduce inter-urban traffic congestion on the motorway network. In proposing a £12 billion spending package, the government was concerned to give support to industry, while at the same time increasing the opportunities for new development in less favoured regions, particularly those affected by deindustrialization.

The government's plans were undoubtedly prompted by the forecasts of traffic on our roads. The Department of Transport estimated that by the year 2025 road traffic will increase by between 83 and 142 per cent from its 1988 level. It is quite clear that, if this comes about, such an increase in traffic will make congestion on main inter-urban routes significantly worse and unacceptable to users, particularly commercial vehicle and industrial users.

A substantial proportion of the £12 billion expenditure was earmarked for major road-widening schemes on motorways such as the M1, the M6 and the M25. These motorways and others were expected to be widened to four lanes throughout much of their length. The main stretches of new motorway proposed were between Chelmsford and the M25, relief roads around Manchester and on the approach to the Severn Bridge.

Implementation of this programme was in general confirmed in the White Paper *Policy for Roads for the 1990s*. Reaction to it was predictably mixed. Environmental pressure groups were aghast at the scale of the proposed programme, while the road lobby pressed for even greater expenditure on roads. A very significant government statement in December 1994 was that, once the *Roads for Prosperity* programme had been implemented, there would be no further major new schemes for the foreseeable future.

The *New Roads by New Means* consultation paper attracted considerable attention in the City. This introduced the idea that there could be opportunities for the private sector to invest in roads, a traditional domain for public sector expenditure. Funding of the Channel Tunnel and the Dartford–Thurrock bridge, for example, was in each case from private sources, but this was the first time there had been formal suggestions that users of roads would be required to pay a toll for infrastructure funded by the private sector. Moreover, in October 1989 it was announced that private bidders were being sought to construct a new Birmingham relief road between the M6 and the M54. Two years later, somewhat controversially, the concession to build it was given to an Anglo-Italian joint venture consisting of Trafalgar House and Italstat, the biggest toll road operator in Europe.

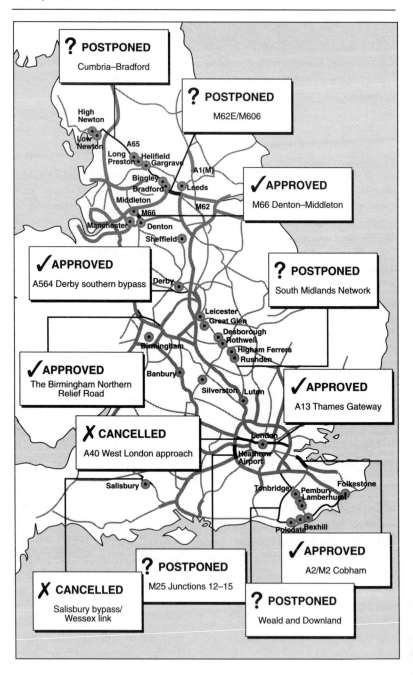

Figure 9 'The road ahead'

Source: *Daily Telegraph*, 29 July 1997

A Green Paper, *Paying for Better Motorways,* was published in May 1993. This clearly stated that congestion would continue to worsen unless there was a change in emphasis in the way road users were charged for the use of roads. It stated:

> '... *the introduction of direct charging could be the key to meeting the challenge of congestion ... and would facilitate more private sector involvement in road provision.*'

A charge of around 1½p per mile for cars and 4½p per mile for goods vehicles was suggested as appropriate, although the means by which the toll would be collected was seen as much more of an issue for continuing debate.

Over the last few years, the intentions of the *Roads for Prosperity* programme have been subject to various cutbacks, in part for environmental reasons but more particularly on account of the now widely held view that building new roads is not the answer to our deepening transport crisis. One new scheme that has escaped the government's axe is the £300 million Birmingham Northern Relief Road, a privately funded toll road. When constructed, it is expected to relieve congestion on southern sections of the M6, currently a nightmare for those who use it.

The appraisal of motorway projects

Over the last 35 years or so, cost–benefit analysis has been used for the appraisal of many major transport projects in the UK. The most widely applied example is in the appraisal of new motorway and trunk road projects. The methodology used today originated from the case for the M1 motorway.

The M1 motorway study of 1959 was a prototype for the application of CBA to inter-urban road investment. Although not as sophisticated, it has formed the basis for development of the COBA model described above. The main purpose of the M1 study was to justify the decision to construct the London–Birmingham section which had already opened for use by traffic. Table 13 shows a summary of the analysis.

The three cost savings referred to earlier (journey time savings, vehicle operating cost savings and accident cost savings) are shown as benefits. The savings in operating costs were split between two classes of traffic, that diverting to the M1 and that remaining on the old route, in this case the A45. The M1 study used this classification to show that *consumer surplus* increased when the new motorway was open to traffic. A summary of this important idea is in the boxed item on page 46.

Table 13 Estimated annual costs of, and benefits from, the London-Birmingham motorway (third assignment)

	£000 per annum
Benefits	
To diverted traffic:	
Savings in working time	766
Reduction in vehicle fleets	227
Savings in fuel consumption	18
Savings in other operating costs	200
To traffic remaining on old routes:	
Reduction in vehicle costs	128
Reduction in accident costs:	215
Total	1554
Current costs	
Maintenance of motorway	200
Costs of additional vehicle mileage for traffic diverting to motorway	375
Total	575
Net measured benefits	979

Source: Adapted from Technical Paper 46, Road Research Laboratory, 1960.
Crown copyright reproduced with the permission of the Controller of HMSO

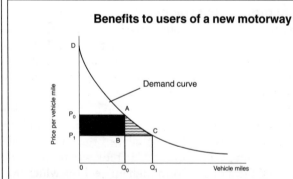

Benefits to users of a new motorway

Assume that DD is the market demand for travel. The effect of opening a new motorway is to reduce travel costs to users from P_0 to P_1 per vehicle mile. As with most demand curves, when the price falls more people will be willing to travel at a reduced price.

At this new reduced price, existing/former travellers will continue to travel. Their aggregate benefit is rectangle P_0ABP_1.

The reduced price also increases the demand for new users wishing to travel. This is known as the *benefit to generated traffic* and is shown by the 'triangle' ABC.

Total traffic benefit = P_0ABP_1 + ABC
Consumer surplus increases from DP_0A to DP_1C.

Looking back, it could be argued that, in general, investment in *all* forms of transport in the UK has been below what it should have been to ensure a quality transport system which will meet present and future needs of *all* those who want to use it.

KEY WORDS

Investment	Quasi-public good
Public goods	Cost–benefit analysis
Non-excludability	Net present value
Non-rivalry	Indirect effects

Essay topics

1. (a) With the aid of examples, explain the terms private benefit and social benefit. [10 marks]

   (b) Explain what you understand by 'cost–benefit' analysis and illustrate and discuss its use as a means of resource allocation [15 marks]

   [University of Cambridge Local Examinations Syndicate 1993]

2. (a) Explain how and why a 'valuation of travel time' is used in the appraisal of transport projects. [8 marks]

   (b) With reference to examples of your choice, discuss why such appraisals may not always cover all of the costs and benefits. [12 marks]

   [University of Cambridge Local Examinations Syndicate 1996]

3. (a) Explain how and why cost–benefit analysis is applied by central government to decide upon major new road schemes in the UK. [10 marks]

   (b) Comment upon the extent to which this approach is valid where some roads are being funded and operated by private sector companies. [10 marks]

   [University of Cambridge Local Examinations Syndicate 1996]

Data response question

The M1–M62 link road

This task is based on a question set by the University of Cambridge Local Examinations Syndicate in 1997. Read the next paragraph and study Tables A and B. Then answer the questions that follow.

In 1992, the Department of Transport published proposals on two possible options for a new motorway link between the M1 and the M62 in West

Yorkshire. These proposals were the outcome of a comprehensive cost–benefit analysis carried out by independent transport consultants. Prior to putting the routes forward for public consultation, an extensive study of the environmental effects was undertaken in which it was stated that 'the preferred route would be the one designed to minimize the adverse environmental effects as far as possible'. Tables A and B summarize a comparison of the two routes, which were named the *purple* and *yellow* routes. The length of the existing route was stated as 23 miles.

Table A Items quantified in the cost–benefit analysis

	Purple route	Yellow route
Length of planned new road	12 miles	10.5 miles
Cost of construction (£ million)	130	135
Forecast percentage changes in traffic on local roads:		
A637	–65 to –55	–55 to –40
A644	–10	–50
A62	+25	+25
A642	–35	–35
Rate of return	'High'	'Very high'

Table B: Items *not* quantified in the cost–benefit analysis

	Purple route	Yellow route
Probable demolition of houses	2	22
No. of houses within 100 metres of new road	65	320
No. of houses fronting main roads which may expect a substantial reduction in traffic	400	600

1. State one strength and one weakness of cost–benefit analysis when used in this context. [2 marks]
2. Use the information provided in Table A to explain why the yellow route gives a higher rate of return than the purple route.

    [4 marks]
3. (a) From Table B, give an example of (i) a negative externality, and (ii) a positive externality. Justify your choices. [4 marks]
   (b) Analyse what other negative externalities might have been included in Table B. [4 marks]
4. In 1994, after considerable opposition from local people, the Department of Transport announced that the proposed M1–M62 Link Road would not be constructed. Discuss the likely reasons for this decision. [6 marks]

Chapter Five

Privatization and contestability

'In every other privatisation, managers have ended up making a quick killing ... in ten years' time, the railways will be dominated by perhaps three big players and I shall be sunning myself in the West Indies.'
J. Harlow, *Sunday Times*, 1994, quoting a likely rail franchise bidder

The position before 1979

Prior to the election of Mrs Thatcher's government in 1979, there was very little difference between the two main political parties in their attitude to transport. With the possible exception of road haulage, which had been denationalized in 1953, successive Conservative and Labour administrations had promoted a national transport policy that had sought to obtain 'Co-ordination through Competition'; that is, they had believed the best way to achieve efficiency in transport was through promoting competition, with the private and public sectors competing in certain transport markets.

At the same time, it was also recognized that transport activities should be subject to various forms of regulation and control; particularly for safety reasons, but also to protect the interests of the public sector (often through *quantity licensing*) and to ensure minimum entry control (through *quality licensing*). There was also financial control by government via subsidy provision for bus and rail passenger services and through the control of public expenditure on transport-related projects.

The incoming Thatcher government was faced with emerging transport problems, including:

- increasing levels of subsidy for the railways and local bus services, which was essential in order to retain services
- long-term decline in the bus passenger and rail markets, both of which had almost complete state ownership
- a freight transport market dominated by road, and where rail seemed unable to gain new business
- growing environmental concerns over the impact of transport
- social concerns over the poor availability of transport services for non-car owners
- a transport network which was experiencing increasing difficulty in coping with the demands placed upon it.

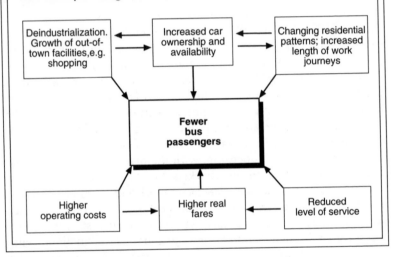

The decline of bus passenger transport

The bus passenger market has been in long-term decline over the last 30 to 40 years. The main cause of this decline has been the growth in car ownership levels, but as the diagram below indicates, there are other reasons related to developments in the UK economy and operational causes which are much more specific to the bus industry. The outcome is quite clearly one of fewer bus passengers.

Deindustrialization. Growth of out-of-town facilities,e.g. shopping

Increased car ownership and availability

Changing residential patterns; increased length of work journeys

Fewer bus passengers

Higher operating costs

Higher real fares

Reduced level of service

The context after 1979

By any yardstick, as the rest of the chapter will show, the structural and operational changes in transport since 1979 can only be described as 'radical'. To fully understand their significance, it must be recognized that these changes were carried out by a government which inherited many transport problems and which was determined to pursue certain economic policies which were based on:

- *A deliberate commitment to reduce government involvement in the economy.* A return to market forces was seen as the best way to achieve an efficient allocation of resources.
- *Public sector services providing 'value for money'.* The need for greater accountability was recognized and the government was no longer to be seen as the 'milkcow' which bailed out nationalized industries that persistently lost money.
- *The need to cut back public expenditure.* This was necessary in order to limit the deficit on the current account of the balance of

payments and to control inflationary pressures in the domestic economy.

It was clear that transport, as one of the main areas of the public sector along with the fuel and power industries, would experience the application of new ideas and philosophies. It also became clear that Mrs Thatcher was determined to break down the barriers that protected public sector transport monopolies from competition.

Privatization

Chapters 1 and 4 of a companion book in this series, *Privatization and the Public Sector* by Bryan Hurl, provide an appropriate analysis of the theoretical benefits of **privatization**. Below, the boxed item applies and adapts Hurl's definition of privatization to transport.

Table 14 lists the main transport privatizations that have taken place and demonstrates how the sale of former public sector assets has been achieved. As it shows, the sale of former public sector transport activities has brought in a substantial amount of money for the Treasury. In the cases of British Airways, the British Airports Authority and Associated British Ports, it has also provided the public with an opportunity to buy shares. There also has been the selective sale of other British Rail operations, including British Transport Hotels, British Rail Engineering Ltd and the 1983 merger of Seaspeed and HoverLloyd.

The definition of privatization and its transport application

Denationalization: A change in ownership from public to private sector
[e.g. bus services, road freight, airports, ports, air transport, railways]

Deregulation: The removal of barriers to entry, which normally protected the public sector, and the creation of a contestable market

Franchising: The right to operate a particular service over a stated length of time, with or without public sector subsidy
[e.g. some road projects, rail passenger services]

Table 14 Transport privatizations in the UK

Date	Company	Nature of sale	£ million
1982	National Freight Company	MBO	52
1983–84	Associated British Ports	Public offering	74
1984	Sealink (from British Rail)	Private sale	66
1986–88	National Bus Company and its subsidiaries	MBO and private sales	325
1987	British Airways	Public offering	900
1987	British Airports Authority	Public offering	1281
1988+	Former PTEs and municipal bus companies	MBO and private sales	n.a.
1994–96	British Rail	Private sales (freight) Franchising (passengers)	n.a.
1996	Railtrack	Public offering	600

MBO: Management buyout also includes worker management buyouts.
n.a.: not available.
Source: Adapted from Hyman, H., 'Privatization: the facts', Institute of Economic Affairs, 1988

Hurl's text recognizes the various benefits of privatization. These are:

- a more efficient use of resources
- consumer benefits – wider choice, better quality of service, lower prices
- widening of share ownership
- a reduction in the PSBR and benefits for taxpayers.

The arguments for **nationalization** (i.e. state ownership of an activity) are also very pertinent, not least as transport was the first area of the economy to be nationalized in 1947. These arguments include:

- the **natural monopolies** argument – the benefits to consumers of economies of scale and the opportunities presented for product research and development where there is a dominant producer
- the externalities argument – where social gain exceeds the private benefit of an activity
- distribution/equity arguments – subsidized public sector services can charge below cost and so help those who are less well off
- labour motivation – the idea that labour motivation is higher under state ownership.

An appraisal of the transport privatizations could be carried out in these terms, bearing in mind also the political arguments involved. Such an appraisal is beyond the scope of this book, although students might consider some of the issues involved for the privatizations listed in Table 14.

Deregulation and contestability

Transport operations in the UK have traditionally been subjected to extensive regulation and control by central and local governments and by other organizations such as the Licensing Authority and the Traffic Commissioners of the Department of Transport. This control has consisted of:

- the setting up and enforcement of minimum standards, for safety, supervisory and technical reasons
- commercial regulation such as in bus and air transport, where the Road Service Licence has been used to limit competition, determine fare levels and the frequency of service.

Deregulation involves the removal of barriers to entry in order to create a more competitive market. It has involved the removal of commercial regulations, invariably designed to protect the public sector, and their replacement with a **contestable market,** where firms are able to compete with each other. Quality licensing, in the form of an Operator's Licence, has been strengthened but only to safeguard safety standards and protect consumers – effectively this constitutes a form of barrier to entry as all firms must have the licence in order to be a potential entrant to the market. (See Chapter 4 of *Privatization and the Public Sector* for further details).

Road haulage was the first transport market to be deregulated in this way in 1969; until the privatization of the NFC in 1982, private and publicly owned companies were competing in this particular market. The same situation has also applied in the deregulation of long-distance coach and bus services. The deregulation of local bus services was different and removed barriers to entry to what was a protected public sector market (see the following box).

The removal of **cross-subsidization** and the reduction of *subsidy* have been important considerations in the deregulation of passenger transport services. Cross-subsidization is *internal* to the business and has been practised widely in transport. It involves a situation whereby profits earned in one part of an operation (e.g. urban bus services) are used to support loss-making services (e.g. semi-urban or rural services). This practice results in companies providing a network of services, rather than just those services that pay their way.

Transport Act 1985 – the deregulation and privatization of local bus services

Scope	All local bus services in Great Britain, excluding London; vast majority of these services operated by the public sector

Main provisions:

Deregulation	Abolition of the road service licence requirement which restricted who could operate local bus services and what services could be available
Privatization	Reorganization and sale of public sector bus operators. National Bus Company subsidiaries to be sold to management teams and others. PTEs and municipal operators to be set 'at arms length' from their local authorities; provision for their future sale
Operator's licence	To become the only legal requirement for entry into this market; consistent with the principle of a contestable market
Competitive tendering	Introduced for routes which were to be subsidized by newly constituted PTEs; all other routes to become 'commercial'
Other	Concessionairy fare schemes to remain available, with safeguards to protect rural services; trial corridors with competitive tendering to be set up in London, otherwise no change in the capital for the time being

It is argued that cross-subsidization is inefficient. The basis for this claim is that it leads to higher costs and fares in some areas, yet lower costs in other areas are not passed on to passengers through lower fares. It is therefore an example of *implicit taxation.* Cross-subsidization can also be wasteful – marginal services may be supported too heavily, generating dubious benefits in relation to their costs.

Subsidy, on the other hand, is *external* to the business; it is paid by central and local governments to protect loss-making services. National transport policy has sought to get 'value for money' where subsidy is paid and has increasingly questioned its need. The days are gone when local government was prepared to write blank cheques to keep bus services on the road and to support services which nobody wanted or used.

Table 15 The impact of deregulation

Express coach services (1980 Transport Act)	Significant early market entry, product innovation, fare reductions, improved service levels
	then
	Cycle of market exits, service consolidation, higher frequencies and more competitive fares on main routes
Local bus services (1985 Transport Act)	Increased number of operators, extensive competition in some areas, reduced subsidy, continued fall in number of passengers, mergers/takeovers and market exits
	then
	Increasing real fare levels, continued drop in number of passengers, fewer new vehicles, deteriorating employment conditions, reduced subsidy
Road haulage (1968 Transport Act)	Strong market growth, highly competitive market, some product development, increasing concentration of ownership
Domestic air service (1980 Civil Aviation Act)	New market opportunities, increased service frequencies, fall in leisure fares, exits from market

Table 15, above, summarizes the general impact of deregulation in UK transport to date. It presents a mixed picture. The deregulation of express coach services has been relatively successful and its impact was used to justify the similar deregulation of local bus services outside London. The reality of this second deregulation has been somewhat different from what had been expected. *In particular, there has been concern as to whether the market really is contestable – in other words, how well does the theory of contestable markets hold up in local bus transport?*

This question is answered to some extent in Tables 16 and 17. Following privatization in 1986, many local authority, PTE-owned and National Bus Company-owned companies were sold to management/employee teams through management buyouts (MBOs). Few now remain, largely as a result of them subsequently having sold on to one or other of the so-called 'major groups' (see Table 17). For example, Stagecoach now owns GM South and Busways in Manchester and

Table 16 Theory and reality of contestable markets in the local bus industry

Theory	Characteristic	Reality
Irrelevant	Number of firms	Declining
Irrelevant	Size of firms	A small number of large firms; many more small localized firms
None	Barriers to entry/exit	Operators licence; statutory minimum exit period
May be diversified	Product of firms	Some diversification
Normal	Profit levels	Very good for a few, subnormal for most
Profit maximization	Managerial motivations	Survival and satisficing in most cases; large profits for some large firms

Table 17 Market share of the bus sector, 1989–95*

Group	1989	1992	1995
Stagecoach	3.9	4.9	13.4
Badgerline†	3.1	5.0	9.3
GRT†	0.6	1.2	3.3
British Bus	2.8	3.4	8.8
Total (major groups)	10.4	14.5	35.9
National Express/West Midlands Travel	0	5.9	7.7
Go-Ahead Group	1.7	1.7	4.3
Cowie Group	0.6	0.6	3.5
MLT	0	0	3.2
SB Holdings	0	0	3.3
Smaller groups	8.1	9.2	4.3
Employee-owned	1.7	4.2	3.7
Management-owned	13.8	16.8	11.9
Publicly owned	30.4	18.1	7.5
Scottish Bus Group	5.7	0	0
London Buses	15.5	15.2	0
Independent operators	12.0	13.9	14.6
Total	100.0	100.0	100.0

* Percentage share of the market based on turnover

† Badgerline and GRT merged in April 1995 to form First Bus, now First Group.

Source: *Bus Industry Monitor*, 1995; reproduced from S. Ison, *Developments in Economics*, 1996

Newcastle respectively; First Bus, created in 1996 through the merger of Badgerline and GRT, owns GM North, Strathclyde Buses and Yorkshire Rider. West Midlands Travel is now part of the National Express Group. These major groups and others have been actively buying up former municipal companies and National Bus Company subsidiaries – Stagecoach now owns eleven, First Bus seven, the Cowie Group six, and the Go-Ahead Group three companies formerly part of the NBC. Consequently, many companies who entered the local bus market in 1986 have left the market, while others have seen an opportunity to make a good profit by selling out to one of the main group operators.

These large companies have shown little inclination to compete directly with each other. Geographically, they are each strong in particular parts of the country. Stagecoach, for instance, has substantial control of the market of South Wales and Scotland. First Bus, its largest rival, has its main operations in East Anglia, West Yorkshire and other parts of South Wales and Scotland. Where their operations do encroach upon each other then in general the competition is really limited; in contrast all major groups normally take a predatory attitude to smaller companies which try to steal market share.

The trend towards increased concentration of ownership shown in Table 17 has not gone unnoticed by the Office of Fair Trading (OFT), who have been asked to investigate claims of unfair practices in Oxford, Darlington and Chesterfield, amongst others. The OFT are seeking to protect the interests of passengers, while at the same time ensuring that all firms in the market do not go beyond the accepted basis for competition. The data response question at the end of this chapter takes up this theme.

Extending the points made in Table 16:

- The market for local bus services has continued to decline, with the greater losses of patronage being in the metropolitan counties.
- The market in London is up slightly, arguably for non-transport reasons.
- The degree of competition for routes has been variable – intense pressure on some routes, no competition on others.
- Many off-peak services have been withdrawn.
- The annual subsidy paid to operators by local authorities has been falling in recent years.
- Fare levels are higher in real terms and rising at a faster rate than the cost for using a car.

Whether or not deregulation has resulted in a better allocation of resources is difficult to assess. Most of the evidence points to this not being the case, a factor which carried much weight in late 1993, when it was decided to stop the proposed deregulation of bus services in London. Deregulation does not appear to be the proper medicine for an ailing industry, seemingly suffering terminal decline. For the future, it has been strongly suggested that some sort of area-based franchise system might be introduced to replace the present 'free for all'. Very detailed service specifications would form an integral part of the contract. Whether this would make it easier for small firms to enter the market is, to say the least, unlikely.

British Rail – a privatization too far?

The main problem faced by transport policy over the years has been to ascertain the place of British Rail in the national transport system. The now infamous Dr Beeching tried to put Britain's railways on a commercial footing in 1963. The less well known Serpell Inquiry, which reported in 1983, investigated what services could be provided for various levels of subsidy. As with the Beeching proposals, the outcome raised tremendous fears for the integrity of the passenger network.

The privatization of British Rail was a complex issue. Unlike other transport privatizations, it was complicated by:

- the loss-making nature of British Rail as a whole
- the heavy dependence on external subsidy for the operation of many provincial and commuter services
- the need to see safety as an overriding operational consideration
- rail transport having its own dedicated track and infrastructure.

When the government eventually decided to proceed with privatization in 1989, it became clear that, in addition to the above, there were other economic issues which had to be addressed, namely:

- how to allocate costs for the operation of trains on particular lines in the network
- how to determine network fares on a national basis.

It took well over three years, and three Transport Secretaries, before the Railways Bill was passed by Parliament in November 1993. An outline of the structure created by this complex piece of legislation is shown in the boxed item on page 59. The major train operating companies are shown in Table 18.

It is believed that privatization will have particular benefits, including:

- increased efficiency, through reducing costs and cutting out waste
- more concern for customer needs

THE PRIVATIZED RAIL STRUCTURE

Railtrack

Originally under public ownership, Railtrack was successfully privatized in May 1996. It has taken over British Rail's infrastructure; i.e. the track, signalling, the stations and extensive land and property assets. It is responsible for the operating timetable, and determines charges for train operating companies and raises capital for future investment.

Train operating companies (TOCs)

This is the name given to the 25 companies which have been awarded operating franchises for passenger services. Most receive external subsidy. Bus and coach groups, other transport operators, newly formed companies and management groups now operate services.

Freight business

This was initially spilt but is now firmly under the control of English Welsh & Scottish Railway (EWS), owned by US-based Wisconsin Central. Freightliner is the only part not under EWS's control, having been bought by a management team in May 1996.

Rolling stock companies (ROSCOS)

Three companies (Porterbrook, Eversholt and Angel) own all of the passenger locomotives and rolling stock. They lease this out to TOCs. Porterbrook is now owned by Stagecoach.

Regulatory bodies:

Office of Passenger Rail Franchising (OPRAF) – has overseen successful sale of franchises. Has drawn up minimum service levels and continues to monitor effectiveness of franchises.
Office of Rail Regulator (ORR) – principal function is to safeguard interests of passengers, while ensuring that the rules of competition between TOC's are fairly applied.

- management freedom to give a market-led service
- increased employee motivation
- less subsidy from central and local governments.

Table 18 The major train operating companies (TOCs)

TOC	Group operations
Connex Rail	SE Trains, Network South Central; French-owned subsidiary of Europe's largest private surface passenger transport operator
First Group	Also involved in Great Eastern Railway, Great Western Trains, North Western Trains; largest bus operator in the UK
MTL Rail Ltd.	Merseyside Electrics, Regional Railways North East; large bus operator
National Express Group	Gatwick Express, Midland Main Line, Central Trains Ltd, North London Railways, Scot Rail; express bus and coach operator, with local operations in West Midlands and Tayside
Prism Rail	LTS Rail, South Wales & West Railway, Cardiff Railway Company, West Anglia Great Northern; new company formed by former bus executives, floated in May 1996
Stagecoach Holdings	South West Trains, Island Line; one of leading UK bus operators, with overseas interests
Virgin Rail	Cross Country, West Coast; part of extensive Virgin leisure and transport conglomerate

Not all would agree. The natural-monopoly argument is particularly valid for a single supplier (see Figure 10). Railways have high capital costs; duplication serves little purpose and capital could become severely under-utilized. As Figure 10 shows, economies of scale accrue in the market, and the LRAC curve has not yet reached its minimum point. Moreover, the LRMC curve lies below it, indicating that economies of scale continue to be gained. The dilemma facing natural monopolies is that they cannot survive as profit-maximizers while producing at the social optimum $(P_c Q_2)$ on the diagram. Consequently, subsidy is required in order to operate at this point.

In the case of British Rail, in 1995/96 – the last year of public sector operation – subsidy in the form of the Public Service Obligation was £1669 million, which was 39 per cent of total passenger receipts. (This sum did, though, include a special grant as part of the transition to operating in the private sector.) Although the sum has fluctuated in recent years, most services will continue to require subsidy under their new private sector owners.

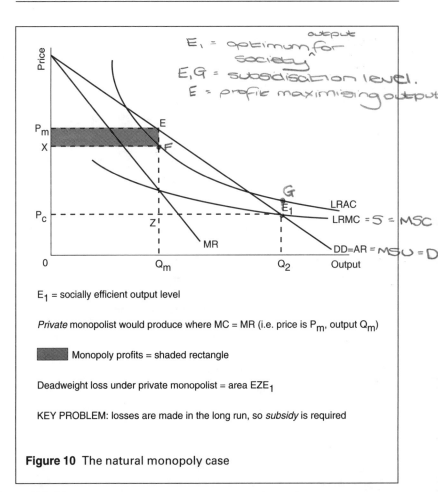

Figure 10 The natural monopoly case

The contrasting forecasted requirements for three train operating companies are shown in Figure 11. This shows that the Office of Passenger Rail Franchising (OPRAF) will pay Regional Railways North East a substantial subsidy *throughout the duration of its franchise*. In contrast, the Great Eastern Railway will *break even* by the end of its franchise, and the Great North Eastern Railway will make a *premium payment* to OPRAF from the year 2001/02. However, for most franchises, subsidies are needed to retain existing services and train frequencies.

This most controversial of all transport privatizations has been completed ... on time! The process of awarding the 25 franchises for operating passenger services started in late 1995, when the first franchise – that for South West Trains – was awarded to Stagecoach Holdings, the

Regional Railways North East: operates local services in West Yorkshire, South Yorkshire, Tyne and Wear and Greater Manchester; lucrative Trans Pennine Express services to Manchester Airport

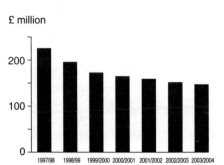

Great North Eastern Railway: operates flagship services from Inverness, Glasgow, Edinburgh, Newcastle, York and Leeds down the east coast line to Kings Cross; owned by Sea Containers; aggressive marketing has seen increase in passenger loadings

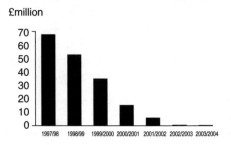

Great Eastern Railway: operates services from Suffolk and Essex coasts to London; committed to service improvement and developing links with local bus services; competing with LTS from Southend

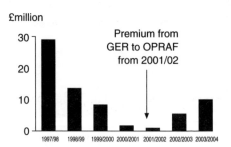

Figure 11 Subsidy profiles of three TOCs

Source: Adapted from *Britain's New Railways,* EMAP Apex Publications Ltd. 1997

bus operator. The last franchise was also awarded to a bus company when National Express successfully obtained the Scot Rail TOC in March 1997.

On the freight side, the American-owned Wisconsin Central has taken over British Rail's freight operations, except for Freightliner, the container operation, which was sold to a management team. After a difficult start, the English Welsh and Scottish Railway (EWS), as the rail freight business is now called, is staging an important turnaround. New business has been gained from road, and business previously lost to road is now returning to rail freight.

Significantly, large logistics companies such as Exel Logistics, the Tibbett and Britten Group, McGregor Cory and Eddie Stobart all now use rail freight or intermodal services in the UK. Major retailers such as Safeway, Sainsbury's and Superdrug have recently started to use rail for primary distribution in the UK. *In short, privatization has been a good thing for rail freight growth.* Additionally, there has been recent investment in new rail terminals by companies such as the Potter Group, Axial and Gefco. In a short space of time, EWS has reversed years of traffic loss and decline.

A full appraisal of the impact of rail privatization cannot as yet be made. Several important economic issues remain, namely:

- Will the TOC's be able to meet the financial targets they forecast?
- Are less popular rail passenger services under threat?
- Will new investment be generated from the TOC's as well as Railtrack?
- Can rail freight sustain the business gains it has made?
- Will even larger groups emerge, as has happened in the bus passenger industry?

The response to these and many other questions remains unanswered. Given the nature of the successful franchises, though, it is most unlikely that there will be three big players when the outcome of the next round of franchise bids is known in the early part of the next century.

KEY WORDS

Privatization	Deregulation
Nationalization	Contestable market
Natural monopolies	Cross-subsidization

Reading list

Hurl, B., *Privatization and the Public Sector,* 3rd edn, Heinemann Educational, 1995.

Essay topics

1. (a) Explain briefly the economic arguments which have supported the continued privatization of the transport sector in the UK since 1979.   [12 marks]
   (b) In the case of the privatization of rail passenger services, do these arguments outweigh those against?   [8 marks]
   [University of Cambridge Local Examinations Syndicate 1995]

2. (a) Explain the economic characteristics of a contestable market.
                                                                    [8 marks]
   (b) Discuss the extent to which contestable markets have been created in UK transport since 1979.   [12 marks]
   [University of Cambridge Local Examinations Syndicate 1996]

3. (a) Using examples, explain what is meant by deregulation in transport.   [8 marks]
   (b) Discuss the ways in which economists have assessed the efficiency of such deregulation.   [12 marks]

4. (a) Explain the economic factors which have contributed to the decline in the use of rail transport for passengers and freight over the last ten years.   [8 marks]
   (b) The government intended rail privatization to reverse this decline. Explain and comment on this intention.   [12 marks]
   [University of Cambridge Local Examinations Syndicate 1997]

Data response question

Deregulation and contestability in the bus market in North East England

This task is based on a question set by the London Examinations Division of EdExcel in 1997. Study the passage below, which is taken from a 1995 Monopolies and Mergers Commission Report into the supply of bus services in North East England (HMSO, 1995). Then answer the questions that follow.

Our investigations raised questions about the extent and nature of competition in the bus industry. In the North East we found little evidence of active competition between large operators; indeed the evidence of several parties (Busways, Go-Ahead, Yorkshire Traction, DCC) suggested that large operators consciously refrained from competing against each other. They appear to take the view that, in what is still a declining market in most areas, if hostilities were to break out between two large operators both would be worse off as a result, at least in the short term. Active competition takes place between small operators, or between a large and a small operator. Table A shows some statistics.

Table A Market shares of bus companies in North East England

Company	Turnover (% share)	Vehicle-miles (% share)
Stagecoach:		
Busways	25.6	19.9
Cleveland Transit	5.4	4.0
Hartlepool Transport	1.9	1.6
Total Stagecoach	32.9	25.5
Go-Ahead	28.4	28.1
North East Bus	16.7	18.9
British Bus	11.0	10.9
Others	11.0	16.6

The nature of competition involving small operators may or may not, however, be helpful to the travelling public. We found examples where entrants had opened up routes which were at least partly new and had charged lower fares than the incumbent. These were, however, the exceptions; in most cases entry led to more services being run on routes which were already reasonably well served, usually close to the time of the existing service and at the same fares. Such competition can lead to congestion, pollution and instability of services as the competitors jockey for position, and provides little or no benefit to the travelling public.

These remarks are not intended to cast doubt on the importance of potential competition. Even if active competition between large groups is rare, their co-existence in adjacent and, in some places (e.g. Darlington), overlapping territories is likely to have some effect in discouraging abuse of locally dominant positions.

There are two factors which appear to create difficulties for the operation of the competitive process in the bus industry. First, it is difficult for suppliers to differentiate their products in a way which significantly influences customer choice. Put simply, passengers will generally board the first bus for their destination which comes and will not be prepared to wait for a later bus which may be more comfortable or may even charge lower fares (unless the difference is large). It is therefore possible for small, under-capitalized operators with old buses to abstract revenue on a significant scale from incumbents offering a more comprehensive and reliable service using modern vehicles. As a result, large operators tend to take the view that the only fully effective response to competitive entry in their territory is to eliminate the entrant.

This leads to the second point, which is that it is easy for a large operator to target a small one. The routes from which a small operator derives its revenue are obvious and can readily be attacked by selective fare-cutting and service introductions. Although entry is easy, it may be deterred if strong incumbents gain a reputation for 'seeing off' competitive incursions.

Meanwhile the rapid process of consolidation experienced since deregulation is continuing. The consensus among our witnesses was that the industry would come to be dominated by a small number – perhaps four to six – of large groups operating across many areas, with very few medium-sized operators but many small ones operating in particular localities.

As is widely recognized, deregulation of the bus industry has brought both benefits and disadvantages. Table B quantifies some of these.

Table B Bus industry trends since deregulation (percentage change since 1985/86)

Real operating costs per vehicle mile	−42
Vehicle-miles run	+24
Real operating costs per passenger journey	0
Real fares	+17
Real passenger receipts	−10
Passenger numbers	−27
Real earnings of bus and coach drivers	−12
Real total government spending on local bus services (incl. London)	−31
Real spending by local authorities on local bus services	−55

1. With reference to the passage, what is the nature of price and non-price competition in the market for bus transport?   [10 marks]
2. Examine the advantages and disadvantages of deregulation.
     [20 marks]
3. To what extent is the market for bus transport 'contestable'?
     [20 marks]

Chapter Six

The economics of traffic congestion

'Jam today, road pricing tomorrow.' The Economist, 1997

The problem of congestion

Congestion is an all too familiar feature of most transport networks. It occurs when the *actual journey times taken by transport users are in excess of their normal expectations.* Consequently it is inefficient and costly to transport users. In 1989, the CBI Task Force estimated that the costs of congestion to industry were £15 billion a year, almost two thirds of which related to waste in London and the South East. Put another way, it was stated that congestion added £10 per week to the average household budget – it costs major commercial transport companies many millions of pounds a year in increased costs and, in turn, these have to be passed on to consumers in the form of higher prices. By 1997, it was estimated that congestion costs had increased to £19 billion a year, an increase of £4 billion in just eight years.

Congestion is not new! In Ancient Rome, for example, chariots were prohibited from using the streets between daylight and dusk owing to serious congestion problems. More recently, in Victorian times most towns and cities were heavily congested as they struggled to cope with horse-drawn traffic, tramcars and pedestrians fighting to use the narrow streets which were totally unsuitable for the new transport demands being placed upon them.

What is new, though, is the *scale* of the problem. Congestion, in urban areas and on motorways, is now an accepted part of the day-to-day problems of getting around. Moreover, it affects all modes of transport, not just road, although road congestion attracts most attention. With increasing vehicle ownership levels in particular, the demand for transport has outstripped the changes in the supply.

Congestion has one definite outcome – delays! Too much traffic chasing too little road space results in traffic speeds falling to as low as 10 miles/hour (15 km/h) in most cities. This is below our expectations both as drivers and users of public transport. Moreover, the air is thick with poisonous fumes; for motorists and most public transport users, simple journeys are fraught with frustration and stress. Road rage and gridlock are part of the complex problem of congestion.

The costs of traffic congestion

Traffic congestion is a good example of **market failure**; social efficiency is not achieved for the reasons stated above. Consequently, the actions of road users affect people other than themselves, so causing side effects or externalities.

The externalities caused by congestion are invariably *negative*; that is, the marginal social benefit of using cars is less than the marginal private benefit. This is illustrated in Figure 12, in which DD is the demand curve for travel. The vehicle miles demanded will be Q_1 when the price to motorists is P_1 (this is the cost of using the vehicle, per mile). The social optimum is at E_1, where price = marginal social benefit. There is over-consumption of $Q_1 - Q_2$.

The additional monetary costs of congestion can be illustrated by a simple example. Suppose 1000 vehicles are travelling along a congested road at 10 mph. The cost per vehicle of this journey is £2. If a further vehicle uses the road, the speed of traffic would fall below 10 mph and the cost per vehicle would increase slightly, say to £2.01. The private cost to the new driver is £2.01, the same as to all other drivers. The external cost imposed on other drivers by this particular driver, though, is substantial (1000 × 1p = £10). The marginal social cost, therefore, of just one vehicle adding to the traffic flow on a congested road is £12.01. It is relatively easy to comprehend why traffic congestion is so wasteful and so expensive when this principle is applied to a heavily congested road network.

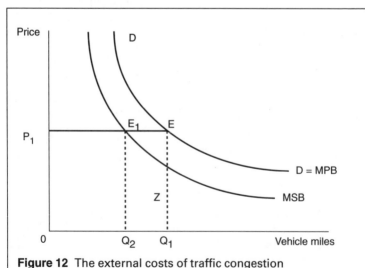

Figure 12 The external costs of traffic congestion

Measurement of the costs of congestion in practice is a complex calculation and includes:

- additional value of time costs to motorists, particularly for work journeys
- increased fuel and other running costs
- reduced vehicle productivity, particularly for goods vehicles
- additional costs to users and operators of public transport services.

An even more complex estimate of the costs of congestion would be if the cost of other negative externalities (arising from exhaust fumes for example) were included.

Policy approaches for relieving congestion

Over the years many approaches have been put forward for dealing with the problem of traffic congestion in cities. Most of these have been planning or engineering solutions, which have little to do with economics and involve the following:

- *Making better use of the road network* – this is a typical approach put forward by traffic engineers and can involve controlling parking on busy roads, creating urban clearways and bus lanes, improving road junctions and park-and-ride schemes.
- *Building more roads* – a natural solution in many respects and one that has been persistently practised in many towns and cities. Realistically, infrastructure development is necessary, but the problem is that our ability to construct, fund and accept new road schemes, particularly in urban areas, is below what is necessary to enhance the flow of traffic.
- *Improving public transport* – this is a logical approach that has been pursued with much more vigour in the rest of Europe, where many cities have integrated efficient passenger transport systems which receive substantial subsidies. With the exception of a few projects such as the Tyne and Wear Metro and the more recent new tramway developments in Manchester, Sheffield and elsewhere, this approach has not been favoured by the UK central government since 1979, even though local support may have been extensive.
- *Increasing the cost of urban travel to motorists* through a variety of existing and proposed fiscal measures (see Figure 13). Increased fuel costs, parking charges and so on are one approach; another distinct possibility for the future is road pricing, which is discussed below.

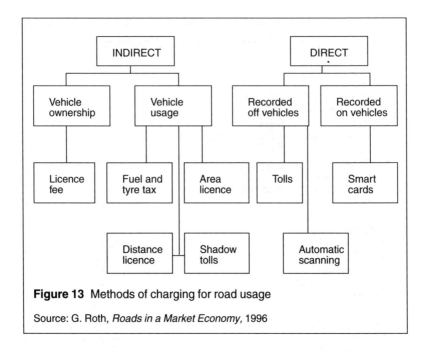

Figure 13 Methods of charging for road usage

Source: G. Roth, *Roads in a Market Economy,* 1996

The merits of road pricing

The basic principle of **road** **pricing** *is that users should pay the costs they impose on others.*

Road pricing is seen by many economists as the only realistic solution to the problem of urban road congestion. The basic principle stated above makes it different from all other proposed approaches. It is also the only one which is economically efficient, as only that traffic whose benefits are greater than its costs will arise. Moreover, road pricing ensures that the prices charged for transport services are more or less in line with their costs – as a result, the market mechanism can allocate traffic efficiently to different modes of transport.

Road pricing should not be considered in isolation – it should be seen as part of a set of measures including those of traffic management and public transport improvement outlined above. It must also be recognised that road pricing is potentially a very contentious issue. A sure way for a government to lose an election is to say that it is introducing road pricing! Realistically, therefore, road pricing is likely to be introduced on a limited basis only – such as the controversial scheme for Cambridge announced in 1991 but quite recently scrapped.

Figure 14 shows the basic principles behind road pricing. Assuming that road space is in unlimited supply and that it is provided free to

No-go Britain: 1996 indicators

Britain's roads, home to Europe's heaviest traffic, will become even more clogged in 1996. Traffic will grow by around 4 per cent, but the country's road system will expand not at all. There will be around 22m cars on British roads next year; in 2000 there will be at least 25m. The cost of the resulting jam to the economy (and tempers) will be huge.

Although many of Britain's motorways have room for more traffic, congestion will concentrate in Britain's economic heartlands, areas

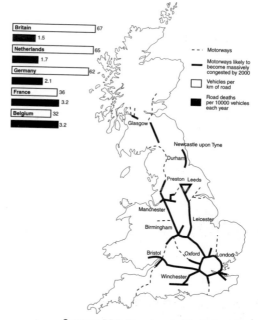

Sources: BRF; Department of Transport; CBI

where traffic jams already cost £15 billion ($23 billion) a year. Europe's busiest motorway, the London orbital M25, serves two of the world's biggest airports. If passengers cannot reach Heathrow, the planes will head elsewhere in Europe.

New roads might solve the problem. But thanks to Britain's vocal anti-car lobby (and collapsing government funding) very few will be built. Even plans to complete a small but vital link from the south coast to the Midlands, bypassing the market town of Newbury, have been delayed repeatedly. Britain's last major motorway has already opened. Rail, too, could soak up the excess, but in the throes of privatisation it is shedding, not gaining, traffic.

Some claim electronic traffic-management is the answer. A trial scheme near London lowers speed limits at peak times; it will probably reach most urban motorways by 2000. 'Intelligent' cars may also help. On-board radar systems will allow drivers to bunch together; satellite navigation systems will help them avoid traffic jams. Government ministers even enthuse about toll roads, despite the likely political cost. But none of these systems will increase road capacity on key routes fast enough. Expect to see some spectacular traffic jams in the coming years.

Source: *The World in 1996,* © Economist Publications, 1996

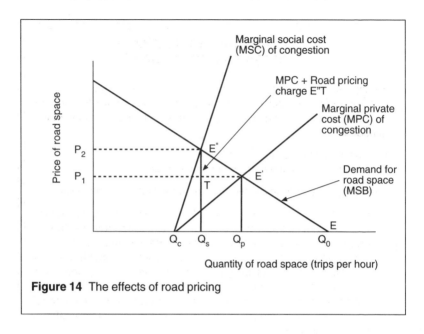

Figure 14 The effects of road pricing

users, consumers will demand Q_0 at zero price. This is the basic market equilibrium. The assumption of unlimited supply is unrealistic – any road has a capacity by definition, which can be shown at Q_c on the diagram. The marginal private cost curve, which shows the supply of road space for users, can be drawn upwards from this point. Equilibrium now is at E', where MPC = MSB; that is, motorists are paying the private costs of using their vehicles. This is *not* the socially optimum point, as road users impose externalities on all other road users, as the earlier numerical example indicated. Hence, the social costs of congestion exceed the private costs – the MSC curve is above that of the MPC. If all of these costs were taken into account, the social optimum would be E'', where the volume of demand is less and the price paid by road users is higher than the market determined equilibrium.

The theory behind road pricing is that the road tax charged to users should equal the cost of the congestion caused. It can be shown on Figure 14 by the magnitude E"T. The additional charge for the use of road space will result in a fall in demand from Q_p to Q_s and an increase in price to users. In other words, the loss of welfare has been removed, so that now MSC = MSB at E".

Road pricing is a particularly good example of an economist's solution which is fine in theory but subject to much debate in practice. In

---

Combating congestion – Singapore has done it!

Singapore has developed a unique approach for dealing with its problems of traffic congestion. This policy, which dates back to the early 1970s, has been implemented by an authoritarian government, determined to:

- limit the use of cars and lorries
- provide an effective mass rapid transit system.

The policy of *restricting car use* is multi-dimensional and involves:

- payment of a massive *first registration fee* on new vehicles, equivalent to around the purchase price for an average family car; considerably higher for company-owned and large engined vehicles
- a *City Area licence charge* payable annually for all private vehicles travelling into central Singapore during the morning peak with fewer than four occupants
- *electronic road pricing* charged on all vehicles used in the central city zone – this charge is made automatically using smart card in-vehicle technology
- a *high rate of taxation* on fuel and an annual vehicle registration fee and road tax; a weekend only discount on the annual registration charge is available; high central area parking charges

Singapore has used the money from the taxation of private cars to fund a highly effective *MRT system*. This is heavily used for work purposes and other trips into the central area. Fares are relatively cheap due to subsidies provided from vehicle taxation.

---

recent years, advanced technology has made it easier to work out the actual cost of congestion caused by the individual motorist (see the case of Singapore).

Road pricing does have certain important *advantages*:

- It is a market-based solution to the problem of congestion.
- It is the only solution to congestion that is likely to result in a fall in traffic and an increase in vehicle speeds.
- Revenue from road pricing could be used to fund improvements in public transport.

Its critics point to certain *disadvantages*, namely:

- It is socially divisive in so far as all road users will pay the same level of charge at a particular time, irrespective of their incomes.

No room, no room

Singapore invented it. Norway copied it. Stockholm spent 20 years and $1 billion before thinking again. Hong Kong retreated at the last moment in the face of a popular revolt. Politicians are terrified of road pricing. How can you get people to pay for something that has always been free? ...

The motives for charging vary. Many countries, notably Spain, France, Italy and Japan, and several American states have long collected tolls as a way of financing the building of new motorways. In New Zealand, road users pay directly for roads through vehicle-licence fees, a levy on gasoline and weight-distance charges for heavy goods vehicles. The latest automated tolling equipment, which deducts charges from electronically tagged vehicles, is being installed in more than 20 countries around the world. The tags are linked to in-car meters which can be loaded either with a pre-set credit or used to log travel for billing later. Charging, aimed at deterring excess traffic from entering cities, is more controversial but is gaining acceptance...

In Europe, road-pricing schemes have been successfully operated for more than five years in Trondheim, Bergen and Oslo. Trondheim, Norway's third-largest city, desperately needed a ring-road to stop huge flows of traffic coming through the centre of town. After much debate, the local council hit upon the idea of charging for access to the city centre, by putting up a ring of 12 toll stations, and using the revenues to pay for the construction of the new road. A high tariff applies from 6am till 10am, a lower one from then till 5pm. After that, travel is free until next morning. There is also a discount for cars with an electronic tag which allows them to go through tolls without stopping, thereby reducing the congestion caused by toll queues...

The Netherlands has a more ambitious plan to introduce road pricing, covering the densely populated Randstad area of the four main towns, Amsterdam, Rotterdam, Utrecht and the Hague. It is due to come into effect in 2001. Cars will have to carry a smart card containing cash credits that can also be used for other transactions. The charge for driving into each of the four cities will be set high, at about 15 ecus ($17), between 6am and 10am, but the price will fall to 3 ecus at other times. Non-payers will be caught on video cameras and sent a bill by the tax office, using the registration details culled from the number plate... There is still some debate about whether the proceeds should be returned to the public in lower taxes or whether they should all be spent on public transport.

In France ... last August, the environment minister was scorched by the press when pollution in cities such as Paris, Lyons and Strasbourg rose to the so-called third level, at which it is generally considered dangerous to many frail people and damaging to the lungs of the population at large. By September, when fine weather produced more smog, the government banned cars from entering Paris on alternate days, according to whether they had odd- or even-numbered licence plates, and made public transport free.

Britain and Germany are much less advanced, but both have conducted trials of urban and motorway road pricing. Field trials in Leicester and Stuttgart have sought to establish how high charges must be before motorists are persuaded to leave their car behind and switch to other forms of transport...

From now on politics, not technology, will dictate the pace of change... As more and more charging schemes are implemented and the benefits of less congested, unpolluted roads are felt, attitudes will change. In 20 years' time, people will look back and wonder why they were ever prepared to put up with the pollution, noise and paralysis of today's cities.

Source: Abridged from *The Economist*, 6–12 December 1997

If you think its bad in Britain ... it is far, far worse in Bangkok!

For the citizens of Bangkok, one of Asia's megacities, traffic congestion impinges upon all aspects of life – environmental quality, human health, quality of life, lifestyle, stress levels and so on are directly affected by the city's phenomenal transport problem. The population of Bangkok is increasing at around 2 per cent a year and has doubled in the last 25 years. As in all parts of Asia, vehicle ownership levels are increasing at a substantial rate, a consequence of economic advancement. In Bangkok alone it is estimated that:

- 800 new vehicles a day are fighting to use the road network.
- Residents spend an average of 44 working days a year stuck in traffic.
- Lost production due to congestion amounts to 10 per cent of Thailand's GNP.
- Peak period vehicle speeds of 6 km are the norm.

The major economic and health impacts are shown below.

Economic impacts
- $9.6 billion per year lost output, and $1.6 billion per year energy wasted by vehicles stuck in traffic jams
- Millions of dollars of additional health costs

Health impacts
- CO_2 and particulate emissions 18 times greater than WHO maximum guidelines
- 42 per cent of traffic police have a respiratory disease
- 1 million people per year suffer from respiratory diseases linked to air pollution
- Bangkok's rate of lung cancer is three times Thailand's average
- Lead levels in children's' blood is three times WHO maximum guidelines
- Nervous strain and stress owing to traffic congestion

Source: Adapted from P. du Pont and K. Egan, *World Transport Policy & Practice,* Vol. 3, No. 1, 1997

- There are genuine problems of estimating the external costs of traffic congestion and establishing these in relation to road pricing charges.
- The technology, although much advanced in recent years, is relatively unproved and could be subject to abuse and evasion.
- The level of charge must be carefully fixed in relation to the price elasticity of demand for travel if congestion levels are to be reduced.

The practical application of road pricing is best seen in Singapore, where a city Area Licensing Scheme has been in operation for over 20 years. Initially, this was a very crude system whereby vehicles entering the city centre between 7.30 a.m. and 9.30 a.m. had to pay an area licence charge. The outcome was an immediate reduction in cars travelling during the peak period and a significant increase in traffic speed. An evening peak charge was introduced later, followed by a scheme whereby anyone purchasing a new car has to be in possession of a COE before they can purchase a vehicle. The cost of the COE is very high and determined by market prices – a figure of $60000 (£20000) was the typical cost of a COE for a medium sized car in early 1995!

Singapore is an unusual, and in some respects unique, case. Road pricing and the COE system are just a part of a much more comprehensive set of transport policies seeking to reduce congestion in the city. It will also lead the world when it comes to direct charging for congestion. The cities of Oslo and Bergen in Norway have cordon charges which apply for large periods of the day, and in Hong Kong a pilot scheme involving the use of electronic number plates has been tried out.

Apart from these examples, the practical problems of introducing road pricing have so far deterred other cities looking for a solution to their congestion problems. It remains to be seen whether the growing consensus amongst transport economists in favour of road pricing will actually be matched by its practical implementation.

What is now clear is that economists, transport planners, politicians and even motorists are increasingly moving away from Mrs Thatcher's vision of 'the great car economy'. The costs of congestion are now so great that they cannot be ignored. As *The Economist* powerfully states, road pricing tomorrow is the only solution to jam today – the ball is now firmly in the politicians' court.

KEY WORDS	
Congestion	Road pricing
Market failure	

Essay topics

1. (a) Briefly explain how users are charged for the use of road space in the UK. [8 marks]

   b) Analyse the costs and benefits of alternative methods which have been suggested for charging for road space in the UK. [12 marks]

   [University of Cambridge Local Examinations Syndicate 1994]

2. 'Road congestion is a result of market failure.'

   (a) Explain the meaning of the above statement. [30 marks]

   (b) Examine the policies which a government might pursue to deal with the problem of road congestion. [70 marks]

   [University of London Examinations and Assessment Council 1995]

3. (a) How does traffic congestion represent a misallocation of resources? [8 marks]

   (b) Discuss why road pricing is favoured by many economists as the most effective means of reducing congestion in urban areas.

   [12 marks]

   [University of Cambridge Local Examinations Syndicate 1995]

Data response question

Bangkok's traffic problems

This task is based on a question set by the University of Cambridge Local Examinations Syndicate in 1998. Study the material below concerning Bangkok's efforts to reduce traffic congestion, and then answer the questions that follow.

New cars are to be banned from Bangkok during the rush hour in the latest scheme to ease the Thai capital's notorious traffic congestion. Some commuters say they spend 25 per cent of their lives in traffic jams. The ban comes a year after the Deputy Prime Minister, Thaksin Shinawatra, asserted that 'within six months' he could solve the traffic crisis that has blighted the lives of Bangkok's eight million residents. That deadline came and went with no perceptible improvement on the gridlocked streets.

Children still leave home before dawn to get to school on time; drivers can be spotted eating their breakfast as they inch their way through a mass of fumes that consist of a toxic combination of carbon monoxide, lead and dust. About the only mode of transport guaranteed to ensure punctuality is the motorcycle taxi service – the fear of being late to those brave enough to use them is replaced by more pressing concern about losing limbs as these taxis make their way between lines of cars and ancient battered buses, with only inches to spare.

The scheme to ban new cars during the rush hour is extraordinary and comes into force on 1 January 1997 when all new cars will be fitted with a new style of orange number plates. Predictably, the ban has provoked intense opposition from the Thai Chamber of Commerce who are concerned about its economic implication despite the fact that traffic congestion is already costing the country an estimated equivalent of £1.5 billion a year.

Previous ambitious attempts to alleviate traffic congestion have failed. The boldest measure was to stagger banking hours in an attempt to get 180 000 cars off the streets in the morning rush hour. Instead, it extended the rush hour and created chaos in Thailand's banking system. Bangkok is one of the few capital cities without a proper transport system – an underground railway has been on the drawing board since 1976, yet construction work has never started despite contracts being drawn up and start dates being set. Unlike some of its South East Asian neighbours, Thailand has never seriously considered road pricing. Transport planners, economists and academics believe it should. With no obvious solutions in sight, the only certainty is that the young men who provide motor cycle taxi rides will continue to offer their unique form of white knuckle rides for some time!

Source *Daily Telegraph*, 9 September 1996

1. (a) Define the term 'negative externality'. [2 marks]
   (b) Drawing upon the information provided, explain how negative externalities arise from traffic congestion in Bangkok. [3 marks]
2. (a) What is 'road pricing'? [2 marks]
   (b) Explain the circumstances in which road pricing would have a significant effect on traffic congestion in Bangkok. [3 marks]
   (c) How does a road pricing approach compare with the other solutions which are mentioned in the article? [4 marks]
3. 'Traffic congestion is already costing the country an estimated equivalent of £1.5 billion a year'.
   Explain briefly how this figure might have been calculated and discuss the implications of this estimate for the Thai economy.
   [6 marks]

Chapter Seven

Transport for a sustainable future

'There is deep concern that the required degree of change in transport policy has not taken place.' Sir John Houghton, Chairman of the Royal Commission on Environmental Pollution, 1997

The problem we face

It is very clear from the previous chapters that the transport network in the UK is in a state of crisis. More specifically:

- Investment in public transport systems is inadequate (Chapters 2 and 5).
- Government expenditure on transport is limited through constraints on public expenditure (Chapters 2 and 4).
- Concerns about the unacceptable negative externalities arising from increased transport demand are widespread (Chapter 3).
- Local bus deregulation outside London has failed to halt the decline in bus use and continues to reduce the appeal of many town and city centres (Chapter 5).
- Many questions remain unanswered about the longer term impact of rail privatization in ensuring that better use is made by passengers and freight of the rail network (Chapter 5).
- Traffic congestion, particularly on the roads, is getting worse (Chapter 6).

Reference has already been made to the road traffic forecasts made in 1989 – see the data response question at the end of Chapter 1. In 1997, the newly created Department of Environment, Transport and the Regions updated these estimates, as revealed in Figure 15.

By 2025, road traffic levels are expected to be between 36 per cent and 57 per cent higher than in 1997. Assuming that no new major roads will be constructed, this can mean only one thing ... increased congestion! This miserable prospect is clearly illustrated in Figure 16. By 2025, chronic congestion will be experienced progressively throughout the motorway network, as traffic levels increase. Motorways in the West Midlands, the north of England, Wales and the South West will experience levels of congestion indicative of demand exceeding network capacity at virtually all times.

In many respects, this is the regrettable outcome of a transport policy

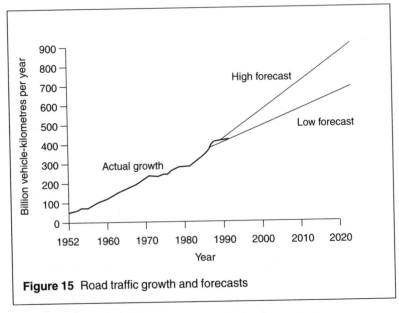

Figure 15 Road traffic growth and forecasts

which tried and failed to meet in full the needs of those who wish to use roads. Figure 17 indicates how, within the space of just eight years, there has been a very significant change of direction in national transport policy. The biggest road building programme ever undertaken in the UK has been replaced by a transport policy which will certainly have a focus on promoting the switch of traffic from road to more sustainable modes.

In August 1997, the government published an important consultation document called *Developing an Integrated Transport Policy*. This clearly stated that 'the forecast growth in road traffic is clearly unacceptable'. Three reasons were put forward:

- Many people who use their cars do so because they are denied 'real choice' – they do not have adequate access to public transport services.
- Increased congestion and the negative externalities that arise are not acceptable from a social standpoint.
- Those who wish to walk or cycle cannot do so because of the dangers, noise and pollution caused by excessive vehicle use, particularly in urban areas.

The economist's concern is that a massive misallocation of resources is occurring. The gap between forecast demand and supply is widening annually, as Figure 18 shows. In short, with current transport policies,

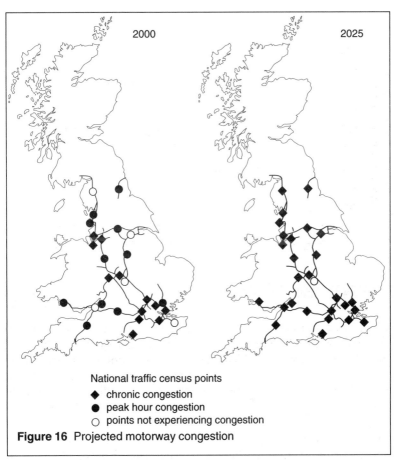

National traffic census points

◆ chronic congestion
● peak hour congestion
○ points not experiencing congestion

Figure 16 Projected motorway congestion

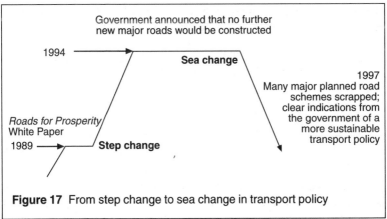

Figure 17 From step change to sea change in transport policy

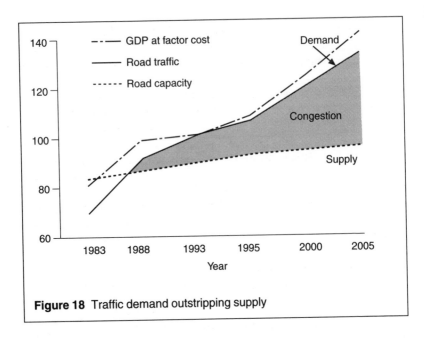

Figure 18 Traffic demand outstripping supply

the government does not have the means or the resources to meet future needs. Change is inevitable. It is for this reason that there is very clear and powerful support for a 'sea change' in transport policy in the UK. The overriding emphasis of future transport policy will be that of 'sustainability'.

Transport and sustainability

The principle of sustainability is relatively new and is one which is being applied to many areas of economic activity, transport included. It involves the application of a deliberate approach whereby *the needs of the present are met without compromising the ability of future generations to meet their own needs*. In simple terms, it means that transport policy today must be refocused, for the reasons described earlier in this chapter, to ensure that in 25–30 years' time there is a transport network which provides for the needs of passenger and freight users.

There is overwhelming evidence that future estimates of resource consumption, CO_2 emissions, vehicle numbers and the distances they travel are not sustainable. Over the past 30 years or so, motor vehicle traffic growth has continued to outstrip GDP growth. With no change in transport policy this can be expected to continue. Transport's share of CO_2 emissions in the UK has also increased as traffic levels have increased. Neither is there enough physical space or government expenditure to meet forecast demand. The wider implications, in terms of climatic change, are worrying and cannot be ignored by those who have a responsibility to future generations. Additionally, the social effects of this so-called 'overshoot' are a cause for concern.

The problems above are not unique to the UK. The question of CO_2 emissions, global warming and climatic change has concerned world political leaders since 1988, when at the Rio Summit targets were set for reducing emissions of greenhouse gases. Transport is a major contributor to CO_2 emissions in the UK – it is, though, not the only contributor. In 1997, the UK government made the bold statement that it would seek to reduce CO_2 emissions by a higher rate than had previously been targeted. If this is to be achieved, there is little argument that it will need to be done through a much more sustainable national transport policy.

A sustainable transport policy

A sustainable transport policy is based on three key principles:

- to reduce the rate of growth of future demand for transport use
- to reduce the future demand for road transport
- to promote the increased use of those modes of transport such as rail, bus, cycling and walking, which are more sustainable than road transport.

These principles are central to the Labour government's 1997 review of transport policy referred to earlier. They were also, to be fair, embodied in its predecessor's 'Great Debate' on transport policy. It is expected that sooner, rather than later, new measures will be announced which will seek to:

- make greater use of rail, for both passengers and freight
- encourage more people to use buses and other forms of public transport
- promote cycling
- make it easier and safer for pedestrians to walk in towns and cities
- increase car occupancy levels by facilitating car sharing.

The focus of how this will be achieved is the stated objective of an 'integrated transport policy', involving better public transport systems, more environmentally acceptable cars and car use, and a more efficient, environmentally sustainable freight transport sector. Integration concerns *the ways or processes by which the individual parts of transport policy are deliberately linked into a policy covering all modes, for both passengers and freight*. In reality, this is very difficult to achieve.

UK transport strategy plc

What is an integrated transport policy? In my view, it is one that addresses the inter-relationship of all forms of transport for the well-being of our prosperity and health.

Years ago, Dale Carnegie advocated a simple method of solving a problem: the first step was to identify the problem. So what is it?

It seems generally agreed, and the government's recent consultation document says, that cars and their associated congestion and pollution are the main one, and that traffic growth will continue whatever we do.

The document does not make much mention of freight, but we in that business should not be afraid to be out of the limelight in this big debate. We know that while some road freight might be attracted back to rail, for practical and economic reasons the transfer will be relatively small and the effects on urban rush hour congestion virtually zero.

So let us all, including freight people, turn our attention to the real problem – passenger transport.

It seems to me that the fundamental issues can be grouped into five areas:

- *Resources:* Extra money will be needed to improve the total transport infrastructure, particularly urban transport, and completion of road projects stalled through previous stop–go policies. This does not necessarily mean more roads, but making existing roads less congested and more environmentally friendly, and improving public transport.

- *User pays but levies ring-fenced:* Car users should, and surely would, pay more according to the amount of use. However, the levies raised as a result of use must be clearly re-invested in infrastructure, over and above current transport expenditure.

- *Shared user transport:* It seems that hardly more needs to be said on this issue. However, investment is desperately needed in high quality urban and inter-urban transport systems and infrastructure, including free-flowing city orbital roads. Private transport providers need encouragement. But work must be done to either enforce or strongly encourage school bussing or school car sharing, and having big users such as supermarkets providing public transport systems. Further, the legal and insurance barriers to car or taxi pools must be addressed.

- *Changed attitudes:* As public transport systems improve, mass media publicity is needed to change attitudes towards public transport.

- *Improved technology:* The encouragement of green fuels, incentives to reduce old, polluting cars, research into engine and vehicle design, along with traffic management development, is essential.

Frankly nothing above is new, and perhaps most commentators would agree with such a broad strategy.

The problem seems to be implementation and above all, money, political will and a government prepared to stick its neck out.

However, the single biggest issue is money. All the ways forward require it, and for years we have been told there is none – and even if there were, then it should be spent more wisely on education and health. But if that really is what we feel, then we cannot expect to have an effective integrated transport structure. So in this debate, let us focus on the real issue, passenger transport and the car.

- *Stuart Archbold is chairman of Archbold Freightage, a major logistics operator based in Leeds*

Source: Abridged from *Motor Transport,* 30 October 1997

20th Report of the Royal Commission on Environmental Pollution: main points

- **Fuel consumption of cars must be reduced**
  In particular, higher taxes should be introduced on cars with big engines, multi-purpose vehicles and 4 x 4 vehicles such as the 3.5 litre engine Shogun and Vauxhall Monterey

- **Heavy lorries using motorways should be required to have a permit**
  Similar to the vignette system introduced in some other EU countries; designed to help UK and non-UK hauliers pay towards the additional wear and tear caused by their vehicles; likely to induce more freight to use rail.

- **Tighter EU limits on emissions from new vehicles**
  Limits which come into effect in year 2000 should be followed by even tighter limits by 2005.

- **Raise fuel prices by more than 6 per cent per year**
  Part of an additional strategy to raise real fuel prices; minor concessions for low-sulphur diesel and other less polluting fuels.

- **Local councils should be able to charge for road use**
  Very clear support for selective road pricing schemes (see Chapter 6); local authorities should also be encouraged to charge for private non-residential parking

- **Improved provision of access into towns and cities for cyclists and buses**
  Urban cycleways and bus lanes should be extended, with particular priorities given at road junctions

- **Greater integration of transport and land use planning**
  Urban design and transport planning should not be focused on car dependence; out-of-town controls on new shopping and commercial developments should remain.

Consequently, the government's target is to achieve 'a better, more integrated transport system', particularly for public transport and to 'integrate transport and land use planning'.

A clear indication of what such a policy will involve was given in the 20th Report of the Royal Commission on Environmental Pollution, published in September 1997 (see the box above). This report was well received by the government and will form the cornerstone of its transport policy for the next century. It is, in all respects, a far cry from Mrs Thatcher's famous view of the 'great car economy' and the current view of Lord Hanson (see Chapter 3).

How sustainable is *your* family's transport demand?

The problem with many of the principles of a sustainable transport policy is that few would dispute their relevance – yet equally, few would really want to change their transport demand and lifestyle.

So, how sustainable is your family's transport demand?

Q1   (a)   How many cars does your family have?
        (b)   Does your family have a company car?

Q2   (a)   Do you or someone else regularly use the bus?
        (b)   Do you or someone else regularly use the train?

Q3   (a)   Do you or someone else regularly cycle?
        (b)   Do you or someone else regularly walk to work or school?

Score 2 points for a 'None' answer to Q1
Score 1 point for every 'Yes' answer to Qs 2 and 3

Score –1 for every car your family has, with a further –1 for every car which is a company-owned vehicle

Score –1 for every 'No' answer to Qs 2 and 3

If your aggregate score is *positive,* then your transport demand is likely to be sustainable.

If your aggregate score is *negative,* then your transport demand is likely to be not sustainable.

Shall we see a great shift in the direction of transport policy in the future? In the short term, the answer has to be 'No', largely owing to the time it will take and the resources, public and private-sector funded, needed to bring about change. In the medium-to-long term, though, there will be:

- a renewed emphasis on the provision of high-quality, frequent and efficient bus and rail services
- a determined effort, through various means, to switch large volumes of freight traffic from road to rail transport
- the introduction of selective road pricing schemes
- greater encouragement to leave the car at home, especially for short journeys in towns and cities, with improved provision for those who wish to cycle or walk
- higher charges for those who drive cars, who will be using vehicles which are much more fuel-efficient and environmentally acceptable than is the case at present.

It is a package of measures like those above that Sir John Houghton was looking for when he made his comment about the degree of change in transport policy required. If such a package, and not just a few piecemeal measures, is the outcome, then the UK will move towards having a more sustainable transport policy. In turn, this will give us a more environmentally sustainable transport system. To make sure this happens is the least that we can do to safeguard the economic and social well-being of future generations.

KEY WORDS

Sustainability   Integrated transport policy
Overshoot

Reading list
Burninghan, D. and Davies, J., Chapter 4 in *Green Economics*, Heinemann Educational, 1995.

Essay topics
1. (a) Explain what is meant by an integrated transport policy.
   (b) Discuss the main obstacles to a properly integrated national transport policy in the UK.
2. Study the boxed item on 'How sustainable is your family's transport demand?'.
   (a) How might you plan an investigation into these issues amongst households in your home town?
   (b) Discuss how the results from such an investigation might be of value in planning future transport policies.

Data response question

Towards a sustainable transport policy
This task is based on a question set by the University of Huddersfield in January 1997. Read the article below, from the *Huddersfield Examiner* of 5 December 1996, and answer the questions that follow.

Enormous cost of traffic jams

It's enough to send businessmen scurrying back to the sanctuary of the office.

A new survey has revealed they will spend an average 13 days a year stuck in traffic jams when travelling to and from meetings in Yorkshire.

And local companies are paying a high price for the road problems – with wasted staff time costing thousands of pounds.

The survey comes from Company Barclaycard, the UK's leading business charge card.

It questioned business people throughout Yorkshire and Humberside before revealing the 13-day traffic jam figure.

For an employee on a £20 000 salary, those delays will cost their company £1000 as year, it says. And it also claims traffic jams could be linked to aggressive driving and stress.

A spokesman said: "The amount of time spent in traffic jams could explain the dramatic rise in aggressive driving. The poll reveals 68 per cent of respondents in Yorkshire and Humberside believe that other car drivers have become more aggressive in the past year. However, just 29 per cent believe that their own motoring habits have become more confrontational."

He added: "The impact of traffic jams and aggressive driving is taking its toll. Some 53 per cent of business people in the region find driving stressful and, among this group, 56 per cent felt that this stress is affecting their work performance."

The survey also revealed Yorkshire business people cover around 456 miles each week and spend an average 36 nights away from home each year.

1. Explain how the £1000 a year cost of traffic congestion might have been calculated and the other ways in which increased congestion affects individuals and businesses. [15 marks]
2. Discuss how national transport policy in the UK has sought to combat the problem of congestion. [15 marks]
3. Comment on the likely policies and contribution that could be made through a 'sustainable' transport policy. [20 marks]

Conclusion

'We need to learn to strike a better balance between the various modes of transport and give people a real choice for meeting their transport needs' John Prescott MP, Deputy Prime Minister, 1997

It is very fitting that the final epigraph in this book should be a quotation from the Deputy Prime Minister, whose Department of Transport, Environment and the Regions holds many of the means for dealing with the transport problems and issues raised in this text. Whether this will amount to a properly integrated transport policy, covering all modes of passenger and freight transport, remains to be seen.

In recent years, professional transport economists have made an important contribution to the debate on transport policy. Through this book, it is hoped that students of Economics will have grasped an introductory insight into the economic principles which underpin the transport problems subsumed in the debate. The book does not pretend to have the answer – what it does do is provide an analysis of the likely available options for the government to evaluate if it is to provide an efficient and effective transport network to meet the demands and pressures of the twenty first century.

There is a lot at stake. In order to meet the challenge as well as realise the opportunities available, transport needs highly motivated, well qualified staff at all levels and in all types of transport business. It is hoped that this book may have provided some readers with the foundation for future study and possibly a career in a fascinating industry which is vital for our economic and social well-being.

Additional reading

The following sources are suggested for students and teachers who may wish to develop some of the topics in this book.

Books

Button, K. J., *Transport Economics*, 2nd edn, Edward Elgar, 1993.
Chartered Institute of Transport, *Paying for Progress*, 1990 and 1992.
Cole, S., *Applied Transport Economics*, Kogan Page, 1991.
Glaister, S., and Travers, T., *New Directions for British Railways*, Institute of Economic Affairs, 1993.
Greenpeace, *Mad Car Disease*, 1991.
Hibbs, J., *On the Move*, Institute of Economic Affairs, 1993.
Hibbs, J., *Deregulated Decade*, Adam Smith Institute, 1997.
Shaw, S., *Transport: Strategy and Policy*, Blackwell, 1993.
Veljanovski, C. (ed.), *Privatisation and Competition*, Institute of Economic Affairs, 1989.
Whitelegg, J. (ed.), *Traffic Congestion – Is There A Way Out?*, Leading Edge, 1992.
Whitelegg, J. (ed.), *Transport for a Sustainable Future*, Belhaven Press, 1993.

Government publications

Department of Transport, *Buses*, Cmnd 9300, HMSO, 1984.
Department of Transport, *Transport and the Environment*, 1991
Department of Transport, *Getting the Best Roads for Our Money – the COBA Method of Appraisal*, 1989.
Department of Transport, *New Opportunities for British Rail*, HMSO, 1992.
Department of Transport, *Roads for Prosperity*, HMSO, 1989.
Department of Transport, *Transport – the Way Forward*, HMSO, 1996.
Department of Transport, Environment and Regions, *Developing an Integrated Transport Policy*, 1997.
Royal Commission on Environmental Pollution, *Transport and the Environment*, HMSO, 1994 and 1997.
Transport Statistics, Great Britain, Stationery Office (annual).

Students and teachers may also find it useful to consult *Global Transport* and *Pegasus*, both of which are published by the Chartered Institute of Transport, 80 Portland Place, London W1N 4DP (tel 0171 636 9952). Both publications provide an up-to-date distillation of transport issues.

Index